Written by one who has "been there and done that," Peter Rosenberger offers caregivers practical advice for everyday living, perspective on their role and relationships, and hope grounded in Christian faith and fellowship. This book is an important resource for caregivers—and for those who care for the caregivers.

Kenneth L. Farmer, Jr., MD
Major General, US Army (Retired),
Former Commanding General, Walter Reed Army Medical Center
and North Atlantic Regional Medical Command

None of us ever plan to be in a position like Peter, but it happens. This book provides help and sign posts for the caregiver! When I was helping to care for a stroke-ridden father for many years, I wish I had had this book to lean upon!

Joe Bonsall, The Oak Ridge Boys

Not only is this a great tool for providing care for another, its spiritual principles are applicable to any situation that challenges us in life. I LOVE the solution of GPS (Grace, Purpose, Stewardship) for navigating the FOG (Fear, Obligation, Guilt) that caregivers experience.

Elizabeth Moss, LPN
CEO, Caregivers By Wholecare

Peter Rosenberger is absolutely amazing. A true leader by example. Hear what he has to say and you will understand why he is the most qualified person to teach you how to thrive as a caregiver.

David Asarnow, CEO Business Oxygen, Inc.

In a world hung up on trying to make sense out of hard times, Peter drives the point home that "We don't have to understand—God understands, and that's enough. He is enough—He is always enough." Peter leads readers through such painful situations with humor and practical help—and in the process, our faith is strengthened. This is THE book for caregivers, written by one with scars and immense credibility.

Jeff Foxworthy

Peter has "walked the walk" as a caregiver and with humility has birthed, I believe, a divinely inspired perspective for a new generation of caregivers. As a caregiver myself, I have experienced the isolation component that Peter addresses in this book. As you read ahead, you will meet an "understanding friend" who will introduce you to ways that can help you rise above your circumstances.

Marianne Clarke, EdD, Caregiver

Peter is authentic in his understanding and awareness when he writes about caregiving—he knows the journey intimately. He is also theologically wise in the midst . . . when he says "we are stewards not owners."

Keith G. Meador, MD, ThM, MPH
Professor of Psychiatry and Health Policy
Director, Center for Biomedical Ethics and Society
Associate Dean, Student Health and Wellness
Vanderbilt University

HOPE
FOR THE
CAREGIVER

ISBN 978-1-61795-382-8

Published by Worthy Inspired, a division of Worthy Media, Inc.,
134 Franklin Road, Suite 200, Brentwood, Tennessee 37027.

Scripture references marked KJV are from the Holy Bible, King James Version

Scripture references marked NKJV are from the Holy Bible, New King James Version. Copyright © 1982 by Thomas Nelson, Inc. Used by permission.

Scripture references marked NCV are from the New Century Version®. Copyright © 1987, 1988, 1991 by Word Publishing, a division of Thomas Nelson, Inc. All rights reserved. Used by permission.

Scripture references marked HCSB are from the Holman Christian Standard Bible™ Copyright © 1999, 2000, 2001 by Holman Bible Publishers. Used by permission.

Scripture references marked NIV are from the Holy Bible, New International Version®, NIV® Copyright © 1973, 1978, 1984, 2011 by Biblica, Inc.® Used by permission. All rights reserved worldwide.

Scripture references marked NLT are from the Holy Bible. New Living Translation. Copyright © 1996 Tyndale Charitable Trust. Used by permission of Tyndale House Publishers.

Scripture references marked ESV are from The ESV® Bible (The Holy Bible, English Standard Version®) copyright © 2001 by Crossway, a publishing ministry of Good News Publishers. ESV® Text Edition: 2011. The ESV® text has been reproduced in cooperation with and by permission of Good News Publishers. Unauthorized reproduction of this publication is prohibited. All rights reserved.

Cover Design by Kim Russell / Wahoo Designs
Page Layout by Bart Dawson

Printed in the United States of America

1 2 3 4 5—BVG—18 17 16 15 14

HOPE
FOR THE
CAREGIVER
ENCOURAGING WORDS TO STRENGTHEN YOUR SPIRIT

PETER ROSENBERGER

WORTHY
Inspired

DEDICATION

Solus Christus

The ultimate caregiver of a wounded bride.

TABLE OF CONTENTS

Foreword   9

Introduction   13

Part I: Head

1. Shock and Awe   19
2. The Delta Doctrine   27
3. A Different Perspective   33
4. Your Decision to Serve   39
5. Hope for the Caregiver   43
6. Don't Believe Everything You Think   47
7. Redefining the Word *Obligation*   51
8. Progress Not Perfection   55
9. What to Do About the Things That Can't Be Changed   59
10. Realistic Expectations   63
11. We're as Miserable or as Happy as We Make Ourselves   67

Part II: Emotions

12. Navigating Through the Emotional Fog   73
13. See the Heart, Not the Chart   81
14. The Hardest Job   87
15. Beyond Guilt   91
16. Fear Is a Four-Letter Word   95
17. Isolation   99
18. Loss of Identity   103

Part III: Lifestyle

19. Sustainability   109

20. Diet   113

21. Counseling Helps   117

22. You're Not Alone: Finding a Support Group   121

23. Church: You Owe It to Yourself   125

24. Why Do Faith Healers Wear Glasses?   131

25. Thy Word Is a Lamp unto My Feet   139

26. Laugh When You Can   143

27. You Are Now Free to Get Up and Move Around . . .   149

28. Leave   153

29. Separate the Person from the Pain   161

30. When Emotions Turn Self-Destructive   165

31. Keep Living, Even While Hurting   169

Part IV: Planning

32. Crisis Management Is an Oxymoron   175

33. Caregiving, One Day at a Time   179

34. Making Time for Quiet Time   183

35. Adding Money Challenges to the Mix   187

36. About Insurance, Doctors, and the System   193

37. Your Other Career   201

38. Unilateral Decisions   207

39. They're Going to Fall   213

40. The Serenity Prayer   217

About the Author   223

FOREWORD
by Ken Tada

Millions of caregivers are out there plodding through mundane routines with hardly the strength to look up, let alone read a book. So why read this one? Especially a book that reminds them of their never-altering, daily responsibilities?

Count me in that group. For more than thirty-two years of marriage, I have been helping my wife who is a quadriplegic. Sure, several of Joni's friends help, but the main job falls on me, her husband. So of all the books I might read in my free time, why read this one?

Because I need to. I was convinced of that after reading only the first chapter. *Hope for the Caregiver* is not a fancy title, but it delivers on its promise. You and I need hope that we can make it, hope that we won't throw in the towel or walk away from our wedding vows. We need to know why we do this crazy 24/7 routine, why we take thirty minutes to order four different kinds of pills over the phone, making sure the pharmacist gets it right. We need to know how much that counts in the long run. Finally, we need to know that a greater source of strength is waiting to pour Himself into our weary minds, hearts, and bodies.

My wife and I are involved in Joni and Friends, a worldwide ministry that serves special-needs families in the love of Jesus. We meet so many couples who tell us they simply couldn't make it without their faith in God. But often, in the middle of the night when you get up to turn your spouse, it can feel like He's not there. Well, He is. And sometimes we need to be reminded that God *is* the source of our strength.

Besides, I like listening to Peter Rosenberger. Joni and I have known Peter and his wife Gracie for many years. I won't go into the details about her disability (or I should say, disabilities), but we don't hold a candle to the challenges the Rosenbergers face. Yes, caring for my quadriplegic wife has its difficulties—especially adding her chronic pain to the mix—but our circumstances have never seemed as grim as Peter's and Gracie's. But that's for him to tell in this book.

Plus, *Hope for the Caregiver* is easy to read. The chapters are short, and you can, with no trouble, read a few pages and then come back to it after running to the drugstore. Peter has taken great pains to make everything practical. Are your medical bills piling up? Is your insurance not covering everything it should? Are you wondering if you should switch doctors? Peter's got helpful advice for you—stuff you can really do something about.

I felt like Peter was speaking to me in this book. Sometimes it helps knowing that you're not alone, that others have charted the confusing labyrinth of medical and family issues. It helps to know that you're not the only one who would really rather go out to the backyard and enjoy a cigar than spend the evening ferreting through EOBs.

This book is worth your time because three decades of caregiving has earned Peter a certain degree of authority. I mean, the guy has been through hell, yet he tells his caregiver story with humor, inspiration, and down-to-earth wisdom. Most of all, it's worth your time because (how can I say this as a husband, as a man) *we all need help*. I don't like asking for help, but that doesn't mean I don't need it. And you need it, too.

Gracie Rosenberger and my wife Joni are true treasures. They are unique and gifted women who have contributed much to Peter's life and mine, and we love them. They are our wives, and we expect to stand by their sides "until death do us part." I suspect that you truly love your spouse, your child, your parent(s), your brother, your sister, your friend. You wouldn't be hanging in there and holding onto these pages if you did not value your relationship with the special person in your life who lives with challenges.

So when it comes to books on caregiving, is there really anything new under the sun? I think there is, and you're holding it in your hands. I hope I've convinced you that this short but powerful collection of essays from my friend Peter contains fresh insights for you. So try it out. Take it to your loved one's next medical appointment and peruse it in the waiting room. Who knows? By the time the appointment is over, your heart may sense something it hasn't felt in a long time: a new resolve to keep caring and giving, not so much out of duty but out of a fresh wind of love.

Ken Tada

Joni and Friends International Disability Center

Fall 2014

The teaching of the wise is a fountain of life.

Proverbs 13:14

INTRODUCTION

❋

Each Wednesday morning, I attend a men's Bible study at my church. With the usual half-dozen men meeting over coffee, we work through Scripture, as well as various theological books. We share burdens, successes, funny stories, and even tragic losses. One morning, I opened a discussion about prayer and admitted that I don't often know how to pray for Gracie or myself.

"What do I even ask for?" I blurted out while holding my hands up helplessly. "If she's in a lot of pain, do I ask God for pain relief, or should I go 'all-in' and ask Him for a total body healing—including legs?"

I mean, we are praying to the King of kings, Lord of lords, Alpha and Omega, the Great I AM. Why do we dance around the subject of prayer? Sometimes it seems that many try to wash God's hands and "clean up the mess." It's unsettling to realize that God is not as freaked out about our suffering as we are. Going further, He deliberately allows.

Some folks may take issue with that statement, and want to put it back on the afflicted. "There must be some sin blocking God's provision," is a common statement. If, as in my family's case, amputated limbs are a sign of God's displeasure at sin(s), then there would be a whole lot more amputees in this world, and in pulpits.

God's use of suffering in our lives—without an expiration date on this earth—doesn't sell well. Imagine going to a crusade to hear big-time evangelists preach that message! That's why you hear words like *victory*, *breakthrough*, and *blessings* instead of *perseverance*, *endurance*, and *resolve*. People want to be bailed out of their misery, and, to be blunt, who can blame them?

That plays for a while, but eventually one has to stop praying for a bailout and start living a life of faith and trust— and our prayers change.

As I pondered on how to pray, and what to pray specifically as a caregiver, I wrote the Caregiver's Prayer. My hope is that it will serve as a helpful road map to a more meaningful prayer life for my fellow caregivers.

THE CAREGIVER'S PRAYER

© 2014 Peter W. Rosenberger

Heavenly Father, I love _____.
I have committed my life to caring for him/her,
Yet I know the task is greater than my abilities.

As I seek to help another,
I ask for strength to shoulder the burdens before me.
Yet I also ask for the wisdom to know what is mine to carry.

I ask for the courage to admit my failures and make amends.
I thank You for Your grace and mercy,
and ask that You help me daily apply it to myself
and extend it to others.

As I walk through this long valley of the shadow of death,
I ask for a deeper awareness of Your presence to calm my fears.
As I glance backwards, may I only see Your provision.
As I look forward, may my eyes see Your guidance.

May I reflect You as I minister to this one whom I love.
I pray all this in the name of Your Son, Jesus Christ,
Who laid down His own life . . . for me.

PART I

—❖—

HEAD

Happy is the man who finds wisdom,
and the man who gains understanding.

Proverbs 3:13 NKJV

Tomorrow hopes we learned

something from yesterday.

John Wayne

I do believe I'm feelin' stronger every day.

Chicago, Peter Cetera/James Pankow

———◈———

I'll never be your beast of burden
My back is broad but it's a hurting.

The Rolling Stones, Mick Jagger/Keith Richards

———◈———

I can't carry it for you . . . but I can carry you!

Samwise to Frodo, Lord of the Rings

Chapter 1

SHOCK AND AWE

When I am afraid, I will trust in You.

Psalm 56:3 HCSB

As caregivers, we sometimes experience "flash-bulb moments" so shocking that the memory is seared into our brains for a lifetime. One of mine came at St. Thomas Hospital more than twenty-five years ago—at 3:00 a.m.

Memories intensify with the engagement of all five senses, and that night, each of mine felt slammed. The bitter taste of old coffee filled my mouth as I hunched over a stack of medical records, while I fought against gagging from the nauseating stench of my wife's fresh vomit still on my clothes. Caffeine and stress fought against me as I tried in vain to steady my shaking hands and calm my heart down after watching her endure a seizure. Ignoring the looks of nurses and staff, as well as the beeps of countless machines and various announcements over the hospital's intercom system, I sat halfway down the dimly lit ward with my back against the wall and scanned over charts, lab reports, and doctors' notes in the massive folder that bore my wife's name.

Despite three years of marriage, that night served as my first opportunity to review the file that had steadily grown since Gracie's car accident at age seventeen, on November 18, 1983.

After her wreck and lengthy recovery, Gracie returned to Nashville's Belmont University where I first met her. Mutual friends felt us a perfect match, and, from the moment I first saw her, I agreed.

"Peter, she's wonderful, but you need to know that she had a serious car accident that left her permanently hurt," one of Gracie's friends warned.

Several others, including her family, repeated the admonition as our relationship grew, but with no frame of reference as to what the caution meant, I plunged ahead.

Nodding my head with an understanding I lacked, I assumed that no matter what her injuries, I still wanted to meet her. My limited understanding led me to think, *How bad could the car wreck have been? After all, she's back at school, and others were trying to set us up.*

As she walked toward me, I swear to you that the sun followed her every step. Although noticing the limp, it didn't detract. This girl was beautiful in ways that I could not express. A nearby friend offered a squeegee to help with the drool flowing from my open mouth as I watched her head my way. Surprising me with her forthrightness, she walked right up to me, stuck out her hand, smiled, and said, "Hi Peter, I'm Gracie Parker. I need to sit down. May I put my feet in your lap?"

Plopping her misshapen feet into my lap, we sat with a group of friends in the courtyard by the student center. Noticing the scars extending above the ankles and disappearing under her cropped jeans, I "smoothly" blurted out, "Good Lord, girl, what happened to you?!"

With a direct look, her frank but understated remark was only, "I had a bad car accident."

———

A whirlwind courtship and three years of marriage later, I sat outside a hospital room in the middle of the night, following my wife's grand mal seizure. This time, I directed the same question to the pile of medical documents in front of me.

*"Good Lord, girl, what **happened** to you?"*

Not even her family had read what I now studied. Poring through doctors' notes, I realized Gracie's accident was unlike anything I imagined. This was no fender-bender resulting in a broken limb that would simply serve as a weather indicator for life. Turning the pages, one word just kept flooding my mind: *devastation.*

Tears hit a few of the pages, as I hung my head in grief and hopelessness. For the first time in my life, I felt a despair that would hover over me for the next dozen years—and one that still requires my vigilance to guard against.

Reading until dawn, I closed the massive folder and sadly noted that the cover stated, "Volume 4 of 4." Before converting most of her records electronically years ago, the volumes grew to seven—for just one of the twelve hospitals where she's received treatment.

The events of that night forever altered me, along with the way I view life, hospitals, doctors, other people, my wife, and even God. Although immature, I was devoted. My sincere desire to care for this extraordinary woman led me to begin this journey. I never imagined, however, that the road would contain such suffering, loss, heartache, self-sacrifice, failure, and love.

My love for Gracie committed me to an existence dominated by constant brutal realities that would end with a funeral, but hopefully not mine. The desire to postpone my own demise might surprise you: I was less interested in myself than in my family. Although I realized that my death would remove me from the daily burden of caring, I also understood that my dying would create an even greater hardship for the ones I loved most. So even "driving off a bridge" represented a poor option.

I felt trapped.

A difficult place for a twenty-five-year-old man.

A difficult place for a fifty-one-year-old man.

<hr>

To date, Gracie's journey includes at least seventy-eight operations (that I can count), multiple amputations (not just both legs, but multiple revisions on both legs), treatment by more than sixty physicians in a dozen hospitals, seven different insurance companies, and medical costs cresting nine million dollars.

As her sole caregiver for nearly thirty years, I often recall that shock-and-awe moment in that lonely hospital when I read her chart for the first time. Somehow pushing the massive despair into an emotional box, I threw myself into the task of fixing that which cannot be fixed, and managing that which cannot be managed.

My wife, my responsibility.

———◦◦◦———

Someone once asked, "If possible, what would you say to your younger self?"

This book is the answer to that question.

On these pages, I've condensed a lifetime of experience into what I hope will be a lifeline of help to my fellow caregivers. These pages contain the things I wish someone had communicated to me.

Through it all, I've learned quite a bit about America's healthcare system. Through marriage to someone with extreme pain, disability, and chronic crises, I've learned even more about perseverance, love, and relationships.

It's not easy caring for a suffering human being— one who lives with a severe disability and intractable pain. I often tell my wife, "You're easy to love, but you're hard to love well."

Armed only with a relentless persistence, a goofy sense of humor, a few "smarts," and a degree in music (composition, *piano principal*), I somehow keep the plates spinning. When it comes to "wanna-be" stand-up comedians who play the piano and take care of a disabled wife for decades, I'm the best there is.

Others may offer opinions about caregivers—seems a lot of folks are talking about this subject. That's okay; everyone is entitled to an opinion. On the subject of "how to help a caregiver," however, my experience trumps opinion.

> Blessed are the flexible for they shall not be bent out of shape.
>
> *Anonymous*

Whatever burdens my fellow caregivers struggle with, I can help. I'm willing to put it all out there. The question is, are you willing to learn from the insights, wisdom, experience, and even failures—gleaned from watching over someone with a broken body for three decades?

If you're gasping for air, you can't help other people.

Sandra Rankin

———⟡———

I have come to believe that caring for myself is not an act of indulgence. It is an act of survival.

Audre Lorde

———⟡———

But the Lord is faithful; he will strengthen you and guard you from the evil one.

2 Thessalonians 3:3 NLT

Chapter 2

THE DELTA DOCTRINE

It don't take too much I.Q.
To see what you're doin' to me
You better think.

Aretha Franklin and Ted White

One day, while flying to Atlanta on Delta Airlines, (**D**uh, **E**verything **L**eaves **T**hrough **A**tlanta), I discovered that flight attendants state the best advice for caregivers—all day long:

> "In the unlikely event of the loss of cabin pressure, oxygen masks will drop from the ceiling. Securely place your mask on first, before helping anyone next to you who may need assistance."

That small directive, which I call the "Delta Doctrine," contains applicable wisdom for so many circumstances—but probably none as poignant as for those of us serving as a caregiver for a chronically ill or disabled loved one.

Compassion and love often mistakenly lead us to hold our own breath while trying to help someone else breathe. But once we make that decision, it is only a matter of time before we find ourselves gasping for air. And, if we are unable to breathe, how can we help anyone else?

Many of America's 65 million caregivers desperately try to assist a vulnerable loved one while growing dangerously close to "blacking out" themselves. Grabbing the mask first is not a sign of selfishness but rather the whisper of wisdom. Unfortunately, that soft voice is hard to hear over the often-deafening cries of someone we love.

Those who "push the wheelchair" serve as the critical team player for a suffering patient. Sadly, too many caregivers don't know how to create a sustainable care-structure for themselves. Simply getting sleep and eating a proper diet is not enough. Caregivers must remain healthy: physically, financially, emotionally, professionally, and spiritually. But staying healthy is impossible if we don't reach for the mask first.

Help is available, but caregivers must be willing to accept that help while tuning out the fear (and sometimes the panic) that can consume us during highly stressful moments.

On a plane, one must simply reach for the mask that dangles. For caregivers, however, reaching for help is different. Most of the conflicts that caregivers experience involve relationship dynamics. If the patient is bleeding or injured, then it is a medical crisis and that involves a different set of skills and needs, generally referred to as triage.

Caregiving scenarios that strain the bonds of friends, family, and marriage could benefit from "emotional triage." Since the one who suffers will, by definition, probably not be providing leadership in those areas, it is up to caregivers to ensure their own safety and well-being. Just as paramedics train to care for an agitated (and sometimes even violent) patient, caregivers can learn to protect their own emotional safety and peace of mind.

When the "turbulence of caregiving" hits, I've found three simple things that help me make healthy and positive decisions in high-stress moments: Wait, Water, and Walk.

Wait: Take a moment before responding. Regardless if the culprit is dementia, drugs, or just your loved one behaving badly, all types of "emotional tug-of-wars" seem to be happening simultaneously while caregiving. If you pick up the rope and involve yourself in a tug-of-war, one of two things will happen: You will win and end up on your rear, or you will lose and end up on your face.

Don't pick up the rope! Simply wait before responding. Rarely do you have to apologize or make amends for something you didn't say. Breathe slowly (inhale four seconds; exhale eight seconds), until you feel yourself growing calmer. Stress and anger are toxic for good decisions.

Water: Drink some cool water. It will buy you time to think more clearly. Avoid sugary drinks or even coffee, and instead grab a bottle or glass of water. Your body needs water—your brain needs water. From high blood pressure to fatigue, water helps a myriad of issues. A tanked-up brain functions better. Drink to think!

Walk: Caregiving creates extreme stress, so when things are bouncing off the walls, take a few moments to put on some comfortable shoes and walk off some of that tension. By doing so, you are truly putting on the mask first, getting better oxygen to your body and brain, and bleeding off anxiety. Walking immediately helps facilitate calmness. Settling yourself down allows you to bring your "A-Game" to the caregiving scenario.

Wait, Water, Walk cost little or nothing but can instantly help a caregiver make better decisions, calm down, and feel more at peace. These are the initial steps of the Delta Doctrine. "Put your mask on first" is the most responsible and caring step in your efforts to help others. In doing so, the patient gets a healthier, confident, stronger, and more "self-controlled" caregiver who can provide leadership while offering love.

Face your deficiencies and acknowledge them;
but do not let them master you.
Let them teach you patience, sweetness, insight.
When we do the best we can,
we never know what miracle is wrought in our life,
or in the life of another.

Helen Keller

Take rest.
A field that has rested gives a beautiful crop.

Ovid

Chapter 3

A DIFFERENT PERSPECTIVE

Perspective is everything when you are
experiencing the challenges of life.

Joni Eareckson Tada

Sometimes, it helps to get a different perspective on a situation, in order for roles to be better defined. Let's start with a few qualifying questions:

Did you create the condition your loved one endures?

Can you cure them?

Can you control what is happening to them?

If you answered "yes" to these questions, then maybe this book is not for you. If you can create, cure, or control these types of life issues, then you don't need to worry about being a caregiver.

On the other hand, if you answered "no" to those questions, you are well on your way to understanding your powerlessness and inability to alter or change the circumstances facing you as a caregiver, and that's a good thing.

Although my résumé as a caregiver is a long and impressive one, I must confess that, not only have I failed to "fix" the situation; I can't stop it from getting worse. In fact, I can't even slow it down.

Mulling over these facts, it dawns upon me that maybe I have a different role to play in this scenario.

If controlling it or curing it is impossible, then what is my job as a caregiver? After decades of putting on the cape and mask and acting like a superhero every time a medical crisis pops up (often daily), I'm learning that my role is to love my wife, do the best I can, and grow as a healthy individual to the best of my abilities.

As capable as I am, it is abundantly clear that I am powerless over her injuries and equally powerless to take away any of her considerable pain. I do, however, have an important role to play but can only serve in that role if I am thinking and living in a healthy manner.

When I first started on this journey, I put my life on hold to help her life improve. After doing this for some time, it dawned upon me that I could not wait for her to get better—or worse—before I took steps to live a healthy life.

"Oh yes, my friend, you would have fought very bravely, and died very quickly."

Don Diego to Alejandro, The Mask of Zorro

When in the hospital dealing with a medical crisis, the normal response is to stop everything and throw ourselves recklessly at the issue. When the problems drag on for months, years, and decades, a plan must be implemented to help the caregiver build a healthy life.

That night in the hospital so long ago, I wouldn't have been able to process a "how-to" manual that required even more of the precious resources I spent every day. I needed something simple, attainable, practical, and able to do "right now."

What does that look like?

It looks like implementing easy-to-accomplish consistent steps to address the six major "HELP ME" impact areas affected by caregiving:

Health

Emotions

Lifestyle

Profession

Money

Endurance

Focusing on the health of the caregiver is not selfish or self-centered; in fact, it is the opposite.

By not seeking a healthy life of my own (physically, fiscally, and mentally), I risk greater harm to the one I love. As her sole support system, her well-being is jeopardized if I make unhealthy choices. If your own life is a ticking time bomb waiting to cause massive damage to one you love, it kind of makes it hard to wear the label "caregiver," doesn't it?

My perspective required changing. Healthy caregivers make better caregivers.

—◆—

Go to bed.
Whatever you're staying up for isn't worth it.

—

Andy Rooney

—◆—

No life can surpass that of a man who
quietly continues to serve God in the place where
providence has placed him.

C. H. Spurgeon

Find out where you can render a service; then render it.
The rest is up to the Lord.

S. S. Kresge

Some people give time, some give money,
some their skills and connections,
some literally give their life's blood.
But everyone has something to give.

Barbara Bush

Chapter 4

YOUR DECISION TO SERVE

"The greatest among you will be your servant."

Matthew 23:11 HCSB

So you've decided to be a caregiver. There, I said it. You've *decided* to be a caregiver. You're probably thinking, *Peter, you don't understand. I didn't* decide *to take this job; it was forced upon me.*

Well, if that's what you're thinking, I respectfully disagree. Since you're reading this book, I'm pretty sure you've decided not to run away (at least not quite yet!). And you still consider yourself to be a "giver of care." So, because you've made the *decision* to participate in the marathon called caregiving, I'd like to offer my own humble congratulations. Here's why:

According to the greatest, and most often-quoted source in human history, the carpenter from Nazareth, you are among a group He calls "the greatest of these." According to Jesus, you're not middle-of-the-pack, and you're not bringing up the rear. Because of your decision to serve, He maintains that you have reached the pinnacle of earthly success. And if He believes it, who are you to say otherwise?

> Everybody can be great because anybody can serve.
>
> *Martin Luther King, Jr.*

Are you feeling a little isolated, or fearful, or decidedly *un*successful? Well those feelings are totally understandable because you live in a world that glorifies power, prestige, fame, and money. In this world, awards go to CEOs, movie stars, professional athletes, and supermodels—rarely caregivers who volunteer to care for a suffering human being for months, years, and even decades.

But the words of Jesus teach us that the most esteemed men and women on this planet are not the widely recognized faces we see on magazine covers. The greatest among us are those who serve. And that includes you.

When the unrelenting demands of caregiving leave you gasping for air, you may not feel like a rip-roaring success. In fact, when the bills pile high and the paperwork piles higher, you may believe (quite wrongly) that genuine success is out of your reach.

When those feelings wash over you, I refer you to a Higher Authority who has already awarded you with life's greatest merit badge. Because you've decided to stay, to serve, and to care—you're *my* hero. And, you're esteemed by God Himself.

Hope deferred makes the heart sick.

Proverbs 13:12 NKJV

———◆———

We hope vaguely but dread precisely.

Paul Valéry

———◆———

You can't connect the dots looking forward; you can only connect them looking backwards. So you have to trust that the dots will somehow connect in your future.

Steve Jobs

———◆———

And we rejoice in the hope of the glory of God.
Not only that, but we rejoice in our sufferings, knowing that suffering produces endurance, and endurance produces character, and character produces hope, and hope does not put us to shame, because God's love has been poured into our hearts through the Holy Spirit who has been given to us.

Romans 5:2–7 ESV

Chapter 5

HOPE FOR
THE CAREGIVER

They overcame by the blood of the Lamb
and *the word of their testimony.*

Revelation 12:11 NKJV (emphasis added)

Every day, I encounter caregivers who are struggling to keep their heads—and their hearts—above water. Oftentimes, these men and women have made heroic sacrifices for their loved ones, yet they still feel a vague sense of guilt. Sometimes, they feel afraid, or grief-stricken, or anxious. Or perhaps they feel nothing at all; they just feel numb.

While each journey is unique, the constant grind leads many to share the common feeling of hopelessness. Not only disheartening for the caregiver, that feeling also bleeds over to well-meaning people who try to console, but sadly miss the mark.

Over the years, others have tried to offer consolation to Gracie and me when they see the challenges we live with.

"I hate what you have to go through, but look at the testimony," is an often-repeated phrase. Another one is, "Your burdens are great, but look what God has done through you all through your Standing With Hope ministry." Further still, we've often heard the *consolation of speculation*. "God clearly has a plan and purpose for all this, or you wouldn't be here."

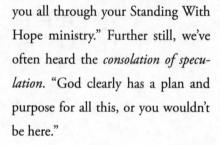

My hope is built on nothing less Than Jesus' blood and righteousness.

Edward Mote

I appreciate the sentiment behind those statements, but they are just that: sentiment, and sentiment is not hope. A great testimony and even a powerful ministry to Gracie's fellow amputees is not a consolation prize for the harshness of our lives. As wonderful as our work is, that is not what strengthens our hearts during brutal times. Our consolation has to be greater than simply doing good works and even having a great message.

The challenges of this world are crushing and will bust you up—and beat you down. We've all seen too many individuals experience harsh events, and then all too quickly promote a testimony of their journey, but then fall apart under the hot lights of fame and exposure. The "testimony" alone can't sustain, and does not offer long term hope.

It seems too many mix "testimony" with "inspirational message." According to Revelation 12:11, they ". . . overcame by the blood of the Lamb and the word of their testimony." Our testimony is bearing witness to the work and it's Author. That's why telling those who struggle that they have a great testimony is missing the mark. Pointing to the Author, rather than the testimony offers tangible hope.

When your wife is seizing, going into respiratory arrest, screaming in agony, or listlessly looking off and living in a place where she can't be reached, no ministry or testimony provides consolation in those moments. What I hang my hat on is far greater than those things—and that's what helps me push back against the hopelessness.

Standing alone in hospital corridors, raging at my powerlessness, watching Gracie grimacing in pain, daily checking to see if she's breathing, or hanging my head in weariness, I depend upon a greater source of hope and consolation than what my mind, and the minds of others, can fully comprehend.

Trust in the LORD *with all your heart and lean not unto your own understanding. In all your ways acknowledge Him, and He shall direct your paths.*

Proverbs 3:5–6 NKJV

———◆———

Worry is interest paid on trouble before it comes due.

William Ralph Inge

———◆———

The very anxiety which arises through your difficulty leaves you unfit to meet that difficulty.

C. H. Spurgeon

———◆———

Let our advance worrying become advance thinking and planning.

Winston Churchill

Chapter 6

———— ❦ ————

DON'T BELIEVE
EVERYTHING
YOU THINK

Worry does not empty tomorrow of its sorrow.

It empties today of its strength.

Corrie ten Boom

Just because you're worried about it doesn't mean it's actually going to happen. We have enough to consider for today. When our fears tempt us to indulge in the pain of things that may not even come to pass, we fight back by avoiding living in the wreckage of our future.

When learning that my wife contracted a terrible infection following back surgery, I grew even more dismayed to hear that she would require three months on her back in the hospital, with multiple operations to irrigate the infection out of her spinal area. Looking at her surgeon, my heart sunk and the fear rose. He'd known me for sixteen years at that point, and he looked at me with compassion while I stated with disbelief, "I can't do this for three months."

"We're not focusing on three months. We're focusing on today," he said while putting his hand on my shoulder.

"Tomorrow will take care of itself."

———◆———

"Give us this day our daily bread" sounds great from the pulpit until you have to live it out every day. Our culture simply doesn't lend itself to living one day at a time, but as caregivers, we must.

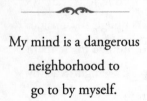

My mind is a dangerous neighborhood to go to by myself.

Morry Ellis

Our minds will play tricks on us, and we indulge ourselves in horrific scenarios that get us worked up into a froth. How much control do we truly have over any of this?

Admittedly, most of what we fret about is "fret worthy," but it doesn't change the fact that we are powerless over a great deal of it. If we can't change it or cure it, then we certainly aren't going to do much good worrying over it. By training our minds, we can slowly walk our troubled hearts away from the cliff of worry and live in the moment—and be content with the "daily bread" we have.

My best thinking took me down into some dark places. I choose not to believe everything I think, and instead appeal to what God thinks about my circumstances—and, more importantly, what He thinks about His abilities.

—✦—

When peace like a river, attendeth my way,
When sorrows like sea billows roll,
Whatever my lot, Thou has taught me to say
It is well, it is well, with my soul.

"It Is Well with My Soul"

Horatio Spafford

It is a dreadful truth that the state of having to depend
solely on God is what we all dread most.
It is good of Him to force us, but dear me,
how hard to feel that it is good at the time.

C. S. Lewis

———◦◦◦———

Thank you Lord Jesus for the privilege of serving you in
your many horrible disguises.

Mother Teresa

———◦◦◦———

In thee, O LORD, do I put my trust.

Psalm 31:1 KJV

Chapter 7

———❧———

REDEFINING THE WORD
OBLIGATION

Nothing becomes an obligation simply
because someone tells you it is.

David Seabury

Obligation is a horrible taskmaster and a poor motivator
for caregiving. Feeling required to do and care for
another often leads to bitterness and resentment. After a
while, nothing our loved one does "is right," and the building
resentment can erupt into painful outbursts that only add
more misery to an already miserable situation.

If you're experiencing these types of feelings, it's time to
reconsider the way you define the word *obligation*. You may
be trying to do too much, bearing too much weight on your
own shoulders, trying to do everything by yourself. When

our hearts carry that kind of burden, it's like trying to push a wheelchair with clenched fists, or angrily screaming "I Love You!" It doesn't work.

Being responsible doesn't mean obligated. Responsibility reflects duty. Obligation stems from being coerced or forced.

As we consider what it means to be a caregiver, we can remind ourselves that we are stewards, not owners. We can only do our best, and then the rest has to belong to the rightful owner: God. Our loved ones have a savior, and we are not that savior.

We push back against obligation by instead cultivating a servant's heart. The loved one receiving our care, however, is not our master. That belongs only to God.

—◦—

"It is not enough to do, one must also become.
I wish to be wiser, stronger, better. This—"
I held out my hands "—this thing that is me
is incomplete. It is only the raw material with
which I have to work. I want to make it
better than I received it."

—

Louis L'Amour, Jubal Sackett

—◦—

The ideal man bears the accidents of life with
dignity and grace, making the best of circumstances.

Aristotle

━━━◦◦◦━━━

I am careful not to confuse excellence with perfection.
Excellence I can reach for; perfection is God's business.

Michael J. Fox

Chapter 8

PROGRESS NOT PERFECTION

*Do not lose courage in considering
your own imperfections.*

St. Francis of Sales

As a caregiver, you'd like to be perfect. You'd like to do everything for your loved one while taking the perfect amount of time for yourself. You'd like to have enough energy to accomplish everything on your to-do list, and when the day is done, you'd like to get a "perfect" eight hours of sleep.

But let's get real. You can't be the "perfect" caregiver—nobody can. And that's okay. God doesn't expect you to lead a mistake-free life, and neither should you.

We will make mistakes, but those are teachable moments that can move us further into wisdom. As you go through the daily grind of caregiving, and as you endure the real-world challenges that are woven into the fabric of your daily responsibilities, be forgiving of your own shortcomings.

When it comes to being a healthy caregiver, seek progress not perfection. Simply do your best, day by day and moment by moment. God is perfect enough for all of us, and if you or I were perfect, we wouldn't need a savior, would we?

When mistakes are made, offer forgiveness to others—starting with the person you see in the mirror. And then, leave the rest up to God. Forgiveness doesn't mean it wasn't important. Forgiveness means taking our hands off someone else's throat—even if it's our own throat.

Keep boundaries, lose the grudges.

We are only stewards and have little or no power to change the circumstances our loved ones carry. Smacking yourself or others around for making a mistake will offer no help to the one we love. If the mistake was yours, own it, make amends, and grow through the process.

———➤◆◄———

Have no fear of perfection—
you'll never reach it.

—

Salvador Dali

———➤◆◄———

What cannot be altered must be borne, not blamed.

Thomas Fuller

Accept the place the divine providence
has found for you.

Ralph Waldo Emerson

We must make the best of those ills
that cannot be avoided.

Alexander Hamilton

I pray hard, work hard, and leave the rest to God.

Florence Griffith Joyner

Chapter 9

WHAT TO DO ABOUT THE THINGS THAT CAN'T BE CHANGED

Accept things as they are, not as you wish them to be.

Napoleon Bonaparte

Understanding and accepting that a caregiver is powerless to make someone else happy or miserable is important to maintaining a healthy independence from the person receiving care. Their state may be awful, even pitiful, but it is still their state and their joy, or lack thereof. We can be polite, caring, attentive, and upbeat, but they have to choose their own emotional and mental state.

I've seen individuals in severe pain who exuded joy and happiness, but I've also met people with minimal pain who exude misery.

If your loved one is miserable, must you be? If your loved one is an amputee, must you be? If your loved one is in a wheelchair, must you be? Their pain is just that: *their pain.* We can hate it for them. It can break our hearts. At the end of the day, however, we remain powerless to lift this burden from them.

> We must accept life as it goes along and do the best with the hand we've been dealt.
>
> *Bobby Allison*

We can and must function as independent individuals, regardless of how intertwined our lives are on the "journey of suffering patient and caregiver." It's not easy, but it is possible.

The key is detaching but with love. Sometimes the weariness and frustration tempt us to detach with extreme prejudice. That's not detaching; that's severing. An amputation isn't required in order to detach; rather it's a simple unlocking. The key to unlocking is knowing the limits and boundaries.

Life has a way of unfolding, not as we will, but as it will. And sometimes, there is precious little we can do to change things. When events transpire that are beyond our control, we have a choice: learn the art of acceptance, or make ourselves miserable as we struggle to change the unchange-able. We cannot cure, change, or control the terrible things our loved ones endure. The only thing we can control is our own thoughts, our words, and our deeds.

You could write a song about some kind of
emotional problem you are having, but it would not be
a good song, in my eyes, until it went through
a period of sensitivity to a moment of clarity.
Without that moment of clarity to contribute
to the song, it's just complaining.

Joni Mitchell

"Then you will know the truth,
and the truth will set you free."

John 8:32 NIV

Chapter 10

REALISTIC EXPECTATIONS

Real life is, to most of us, a perpetual compromise
between the ideal and the possible.

Bertrand Russell

For many caregivers, facing reality is difficult. After all, we want our loved ones to find healing. As we wish-and-wait for their recovery, we're tempted to set unrealistic expectations for ourselves and for our loved ones. When we do, we're setting everybody up for biggie-sized portions of frustration and disappointment.

It's taken me many years to discover and admit that I am powerless over Gracie's challenges. Despite my love for her, and despite my best efforts, I cannot take away her chronic pain. I desperately wish that I could, but I can't.

As a double-amputee with prosthetic limbs, Gracie falls on occasion. I can't prevent it, and it breaks my heart when it happens.

But it's reality. And in my better moments, I accept our world as it is, not as I wish it would be. I've come to appreciate realistic expectations. Reality can be a tough companion at times, but it's an honest friend.

Facing reality doesn't mean abandoning hope. And it doesn't mean giving up.

Facing reality means accepting the world as it is. As we do so, it's important to remember that as we face the caregiver's reality, we can accept that world while also working to make it a little better for at least two people: ourselves and our loved ones.

—◆—

Life is not a problem to be solved,
but a reality to be experienced.

—

Søren Kierkegaard

—◆—

Finally brothers, whatever is true,
whatever is honorable,
whatever is just, whatever is pure,
whatever is lovely, whatever is commendable—
if there is any moral excellence and if there is any praise—
dwell on these things.

Philippians 4:8 HCSB

⸻

If you carry joy in your heart,
you can heal any moment.

Carlos Santana

⸻

The trouble with many men is that they have
got just enough religion to make them miserable.
If there is not joy in religion,
you have got a leak in your religion.

Billy Sunday

Chapter 11

WE'RE AS MISERABLE OR
AS HAPPY AS WE MAKE
OURSELVES

Nehemiah said, "Go and enjoy choice food and sweet drinks,
and send some to those who have nothing prepared.
This day is sacred to our Lord. Do not grieve,
for the joy of the LORD is your strength."

Nehemiah 8:10 NIV

I've seen joyful caregivers, and I've seen miserable ones. For the joyful ones, I think, that the ones who abandoned their desire to be CEO of the universe tend to exercise their newfound freedom with joy. It's a terrible thing to feel as if you have to be in charge of everything.

Here's a simple test: Look down at your hands. Do you see nail prints?

No? Well, good news: you're not in charge. That realization means that you don't have to carry things that aren't yours.

They're going to bleed.
They're going to fall.
They're going to suffer.
They're going to die.

You cannot stop those things from happening. Spending your life trying to stave off the inevitable is the fastest route to bitterness, resentment, hopelessness, and even insanity.

Spending your days doing what you have control over (your thoughts, words, and deeds) and leaving the rest to God is the only way to peace, calmness, and yes, joy.

Joy is not the absence of challenges and pain: that's numbness. Gracie can be out of pain today, but she would be numb from anesthesia drugs. Would her joy increase?

I once quoted Gracie in a song I wrote,

"Sometimes the pain each day can bring
clouds the joy that is there."

"The Love of Jesus," Peter W. Rosenberger and Hank Martin

There is joy; there is happiness. Pain and heartache can only cloud it, not remove it. Our challenge then becomes, will we choose to trust that joy is there when it's not seen or felt?

I've learned that even when all of your senses are screaming at you, joy is still there. If we allow it to, joy can even hold us as we grieve.

The moment you choose to slip your scared hand into His scarred hand, you are embracing something that transcends the pain you currently face. Even in the sorrow each day brings, there waits a joy beyond our understanding.

PART II

❈

EMOTIONS

The cheerful heart has a continual feast.

Proverbs 15:15 NIV

I take my emotions and funnel them
into something positive.

Brian Wilson

The spiritual life is a life beyond moods.
It is a life in which we choose joy and do not allow
ourselves to become victims of passing feelings
of happiness or depression.

Henri Nouwen

———⋅◆⋅———

*"Well done, good and faithful servant; you were faithful
over a few things, I will make you ruler over many things.
Enter into the joy of your lord."*

Matthew 25:21 NKJV

Chapter 12

NAVIGATING THROUGH THE EMOTIONAL FOG

There are good and there are bad times, but our mood changes more often than our fortune.

Jules Renard

Caregivers bounce all over the emotional map between compassion and frustration, between obligation and commitment. The lines get so blurry at times, that caregivers often find themselves operating out of intense Fear, Obligation, and Guilt . . . which leads to Heartache, Anger, and Turmoil.

Get it? In a FOG with a HAT? FOG HAT! (I like '70's music.)

How do ships and planes navigate through a FOG? They use a GPS (Global Positioning System), of course. So, why not people?

FEAR

OBLIGATION

GUILT

Can be navigated by using a **GPS**

GRACE

PURPOSE

STEWARDSHIP

Human emotions are highly variable, decidedly un-predictable, and often unreliable. Our emotions are like the weather, only far more fickle. So we must learn to live by faith, not by the ups and downs of our own emotional roller coasters.

Who is in charge of your emotions? Is it you? Or have you formed the unfortunate habit of letting other people—or troubling situations—determine the quality of your thoughts and the direction of your day?

As a caregiver with big responsibilities, you owe it to yourself *and* your loved one to learn how to control your emotions before your emotions control you.

Sometime soon, you will probably be gripped by negative emotions (think FOG HAT), and at first, you'll believe everything you think. Take the time to catch yourself before those emotions run wild. To navigate through your emotional fog, use God's GPS (Grace, Purpose, and Stewardship). And while you're at it, turn the ultimate outcome over to God.

Your emotions will inevitably change; God will not. I recall a farmer in Ghana named Kwame who received a prosthetic limb from our organization, Standing With Hope. The entire time we made the limb, he complained about his amputation. After receiving his prosthesis from us, I sat down with him and offered, "Kwame, I know you are bitter about the loss of your leg. I know that you blame God for allowing the amputation." Motioning to Gracie across the room, I also pointed to the high performance prosthetic foot on Kwame's new prosthesis. "Kwame, that foot belonged to my wife. She gave one of her prosthetic feet so that you could walk. She trusted God with the loss of both of her legs, and now you are literally able to stand . . . on her faith." As he looked at me with widening eyes, I added, "Each step you take, I want you to remember you are doing so on her faith."

Kwame started a life of trusting God, one footstep at a time. Within a short time, he was walking, and even running.

How is our journey any different? Today is a good day to take one step of faith . . . and trust that God is working in your life and circumstances in ways that you can't possibly imagine.

More Thoughts about Your Personal GPS and about Grace

My grace is sufficient for you, for My strength
is made perfect in weakness.

2 Corinthians 12:9 NKJV

———◆———

The grace of God is sufficient for all our needs, for every
problem, and for every difficulty, for every broken heart,
and for every human sorrow.

Peter Marshall

———◆———

God's grace is just the right amount of just the right quality
arriving as if from nowhere at just the right time.

Bill Bright

———◆———

Let us therefore come boldly to the throne of grace, that we may
obtain mercy and find grace to help in time of need.

Hebrews 4:16 NKJV

About Purpose

First say to yourself what you would be;
then do what you have to do.

Epictetus

———

You're the only one who can do what you do.

Lois Evans

———

Do something worth remembering.

Elvis Presley

———

*For it is God who is working in you,
enabling you both to desire and to work out His good purpose.*

Philippians 2:13 HCSB

About Stewardship

As each one has received a gift, minister it to one another,
as good stewards of the manifold grace of God.

1 Peter 4:10 NKJV

—◦◦◦—

Employ whatever God has entrusted you with,
in doing good, all possible good,
in every possible kind and degree.

John Wesley

—◦◦◦—

God doesn't want your ability—he wants your availability.

Bobby Bowden

—◦◦◦—

When he was young, I told Dale Jr. that hunting and
racing are a lot alike. Holding that steering wheel and
holding that rifle both mean you better be responsible.

Dale Earnhardt

You must look in to other people—as well as at them.

Lord Chesterfield

———✦———

Love is a great beautifier.

Louisa May Alcott

———✦———

Love is patient, love is kind and is not jealous;
love does not brag and is not arrogant, does not act
unbecomingly; it does not seek its own, is not provoked,
does not take into account a wrong suffered, does not rejoice
in unrighteousness, but rejoices with the truth; bears all things,
believes all things, hopes all things, endures all things.

1 Corinthians 13:4–7 NASB

Chapter 13

SEE THE HEART, NOT THE CHART

I pray that your love for each other will overflow more
and more, and that you will keep on growing
in your knowledge and understanding.

Philippians 1:9 NLT

Sometimes, caregiving seems to be an all-consuming task. The magnitude of the job places such a strain on the relationship that the tender flower of love is often crushed under the massive weight of daily medical crises. Although triage, medical procedures, and medically related tasks are important, they are *not* the relationship. The cry of the heart is often drowned by the moan of the body, and it takes time and practice to differentiate between the two.

When you find that the entire conversation revolves around medical information, that's a clear indicator that the matters of the heart are being shoved aside. Use that moment to look beyond the tubes, beyond the casts, the wheelchairs, the colostomies, the prosthetic limbs, the pills, and all the other distractions. Ignore the treatments and look, instead, at the person.

When Jesus healed the paralyzed man lowered through the roof, He first addressed the condition of his heart by forgiving his sins. He saw past the medical circumstances and spoke to the greater need of the heart.

We can model that, if we choose. It's rarely easy, and it will cost us our dignity, pride, and ego. Loving someone has that effect. The one we care for may not recognize or even appreciate what we do on their behalf, and that's okay— if we love them, we're doing it for their benefit not ours. Being angry while trying to care for them isn't helpful or sustainable; it's about keeping our hearts tender—while seeing their heart.

Keeping our hearts tender is not easy. Caregiving contains many flashpoints, and it's all too easy to pop off and say and do hurtful things. We often find ourselves at the breaking point, and that makes it exponentially harder to focus on the relationship with our loved one, when our emotions are already fried.

A caller to my radio show once asked, "How can I communicate to my loved one that I can't handle it anymore— that it's coming off the rails?"

My reply was, "The person who needs to hear it's coming off the rails is not your loved one . . . it's you—and preferably in the presence of a counselor."

We can't take for granted that the one we care for can understand our frustration. My brother has a twenty-six-year-old daughter born with cerebral palsy and severe cognitive impairments. Taking care of her is like caring for a giant baby. Kelsey cannot process what my brother and sister-in-law go through. She just lives her life.

Developmental issues, narcotics, alcohol, or a variety of other impairments may prevent an empathy towards your circumstances. Chronic pain and disease have a way of blocking the field of view for folks, and all they can see is their own need. Some days, quite bluntly, they're just having a bad day and, even if they could, they won't process your feelings.

Reacting to their behavior will only heap more frustration, rage, and ultimately guilt upon you. Don't put yourself in a position to fight with them, and regardless of how they behave, we never get a "free pass to be an ass." It's okay to detach from those feelings and their behavior. As you learn to serve for a higher reason than just the immediate, you will find that you can respond without reacting.

If they are abusive, then professionals (physicians, counselors, and even law enforcement) may need to be contacted. If, however, they are behaving poorly try to remember that they are not doing it to you; they're just doing it. Some level of impairment or personality issue is driving their behavior.

You can still see past all of that and minister to the heart, and you don't have to go to every fight that you get a ticket to—you can sit a few of them out.

When cleaning up a mess or dressing a wound, I'd rather weep than grind my teeth.

I find it helps me to think about how Christ willingly endured the cross on my behalf.

—◦—

Christian love, either towards God or
towards man, is an affair of the will.

—

C. S. Lewis

—◦—

For I have learned in whatever situation I am to be content.
I know how to be brought low, and I know how to abound.
In any and every circumstance, I have learned the secret
of facing plenty and hunger, abundance and need. I can do
all things through him who strengthens me.

Philippians 4:11–13 ESV

———◦◦◦———

The world ain't all sunshine and rainbows.
It's a very mean and nasty place and I don't care
how tough you are it will beat you to your knees and
keep you there permanently if you let it. You, me,
or nobody is gonna hit as hard as life. But it ain't about
how hard you hit. It's about how hard you can get hit
and keep moving forward. How much you can take
and keep moving forward. That's how winning is done!

Sylvester Stallone as Rocky Balboa

Chapter 14

THE HARDEST JOB

Indeed we count them blessed who endure.

James 5:11 NKJV

Serving as a caregiver remains the hardest task I've ever accepted. With so many conflicting emotions, finding peace sometimes seems impossible. Torn between a deep love for my spouse and the thorny feelings associated with constant caring for the needs of another human being, I often close my eyes and think of a happy place. But sometimes, I still see myself decades ago at that hospital, hunched over Gracie's chart, covered with vomit, and my eyes filling with tears.

Mistakes? Oh, I've had ample time to make just about every kind of mistake one can. I've forgotten more mistakes than most caregivers will ever make. Yet, even those missteps can serve as valuable lessons to help shape how I deal with the stresses and challenges of caregiving.

I suppose that crying, "Help me!" is the first step in improving your life as a caregiver. But if you're one of those self-reliant, do-it-yourself, rugged individuals who doesn't like to ask for help, you may find it difficult to ask for the assistance you need, even when you're feeling overwhelmed.

Caregiving may be the hardest job you'll ever tackle. Don't try to tackle it alone. And don't try to tackle it by denying yourself the care you need to do the job right.

In almost thirty years of caregiving, I've learned many lessons. And I'm still learning. Most of all, I'm learning that although there are many things beyond my ability to change, I, however, can change. If nothing else, I am making progress at being content in the middle of very unsettling things. While far away from perfection, I am encouraged by the changes and personal growth I often glimpse.

———◦———

They're not doing it to you,
they're just doing it.

—

Anonymous

———◦———

Let's take Jesus at his word.
When he says we're forgiven, let's unload the guilt.
When he says we're valuable, let's believe him.
When he says we're eternal, let's bury our fear.
When he says we're provided for, let's stop worrying.

Max Lucado

But they whose guilt within their bosoms lie
Imagine every eye beholds their blame.

Shakespeare

Guilt is the gift that keeps on giving.

Erma Bombeck

For the LORD your God is a merciful God. . . .

Deuteronomy 4:31 NIV

Chapter 15

BEYOND GUILT

Calvin: "There's no problem so awful, that you can't add
some guilt to it and make it even worse."

Bill Watterson,

The Complete Calvin and Hobbes

Guilt comes from many sources, not just the big-time
sins that get great press. So it's not surprising that
caregivers, who make heroic sacrifices every day, still struggle
mightily with guilt.

Being able to get up and walk while our loved one can't;
jumping into the car to run errands while he or she is stuck
at home; standing up in the shower while the other person
must use the shower bench; being pain-free, while the loved
one never knows a day without suffering. These are just a few
examples of the guilt-inducing situations that may plague
caregivers. And parents of disabled children may wrestle with

intense guilt over the condition of sons or daughters born with physical or mental limitations they didn't ask for and can't fully understand.

In addition, we caregivers make mistakes, some of them grievous. We are, after all, fallible—and often exhausted—human beings. We trip over the same sins and vices that others do, but the immense pressure of caregiving often compresses our learning curve.

Most individuals experience a "slow growth" into maturity and life crises. But, as caregivers, we often find ourselves in life's "express lane," managing crisis after crisis, sometimes dealing with life-and-death issues. The stress from the nonstop barrage dulls our senses, and may even eat away at our moral compass. When we do fail, guilt from the failure gnaws at the soul. So we work even harder, denying ourselves more, thus adding more pressures to our already-stress-filled lives.

But guilt is not the answer. Guilt doesn't strengthen relationships; it destroys them. Caregivers can't effectively live and serve others while bearing so heavy a burden of shame or guilt.

So, we must apply grace to those guilty feelings. By consistently reminding ourselves that God's grace covers our sins, we discover that guilt no longer whips us into a frenzy. Grace frees us to love and to serve with a clean heart. Sometimes, remembering God's grace is not a day-to-day thing; it's a minute-to-minute lifeline.

———

My sin, oh, the bliss of this glorious thought!
My sin, not in part but the whole,
Is nailed to the cross, and I bear it no more,
Praise the Lord, praise the Lord, O my soul!

"It Is Well with My Soul"

Horatio Spafford

"In time, we hate that which we often fear."

William Shakespeare, Antony and Cleopatra

———◆———

"Be strong and courageous, and do the work.
Do not be afraid or discouraged,
for the LORD God, my God, is with you."

1 Chronicles 28:20 NIV

Chapter 16

FEAR IS A FOUR-LETTER WORD

No one ever told me that grief felt so like fear.

C. S. Lewis, A Grief Observed

Caregiving is not for the faint of heart. The demands are great; the stakes are high; the dangers are real, and, sometimes, so is the fear.

As a caregiver, you live in a world that can be a frightening place—and often, a discouraging place. You live in a world where life-changing losses can be painful and profound. But, with God's help, you can meet those challenges with confidence and calmness.

Many of the things we worry about never come to pass, yet we worry still. Worrying is indulging ourselves in the pain of things that may never happen. We worry about the future and the past; we worry about money, doctors, and insurance. As we survey the landscape of our lives, we observe all manner of molehills and we imagine them to be mountains. Sometimes, the mountains we see are real, but often they're not.

Are you concerned about the inevitable challenges of caregiving? If so, why not ask God to help you regain a clear perspective about the obstacles (and opportunities) that confront you? When you ask Him for help, He can touch your heart, clear your vision, renew your mind, and calm your fears.

During the darker days of life, we are wise to remember the words of Jesus, who reassured His disciples saying, "Take courage! It is I. Don't be afraid" (Matt. 14:27 NIV).

Peppered throughout the Bible, God continually reminds individuals and groups to "not be afraid." He knows that as we face things in life, we are scared spitless. He doesn't mock our fear; He calms it with His presence. Then, with God's comfort and His love in our hearts, we can offer encouragement to others. And by helping them face *their* fears, we can, in turn, tackle our own challenges with courage, determination, and faith. Feeling out of control scares us. Learning we don't have to be, relieves us.

———⊰⊱———

The LORD is the One who will go before you.
He will be with you; He will not leave you or
forsake you. Do not be afraid or discouraged.

—

Deuteronomy 31:8 HCSB

———⊰⊱———

All the lonely people, where do they all come from?

All the lonely people, where do they all belong?

"Eleanor Rigby," Paul McCartney/John Lennon

Abide with me; fast falls the eventide;

The darkness deepens; Lord, with me abide;

When other helpers fail and comforts flee,

Help of the helpless, oh, abide with me.

"Abide with Me," Henry Francis Lyte

Do not be inaccessible. None is so perfect that

he does not need at times the advice of others.

Baltasar Gracián

We cannot live only for ourselves.

A thousand fibers connect us with our fellow men.

Herman Melville

Chapter 17

ISOLATION

*Loneliness is the first thing which
God's eye named not good.*

John Milton

At the onset of the condition, friends, family members, and others usually surround the situation with love, meals, kindness, and attention. As time progresses, relationships wax and wane—and new faces appear on the scene. But when the months drag into years (and even decades), relationships often fade, and a feeling of isolation may envelope the caregiver. Other people may simply not know the needs, or perhaps they can't find the words, or the situation just seems too uncomfortable to get involved.

Regardless of the reasons, time has a way of filtering relationships, and the caregiver is left to fend alone without meaningful interaction outside of a bleak situation that, at best, stays the same for long stretches. At worst, the situation deteriorates. If the condition worsens, more individuals may appear on the scene to provide additional help, but the increased level of support may also mean that a new plateau of loss is imminent.

Isolation often occurs due to logistics. Sometimes, it is not possible or practical for the caregiver to transport the loved one outside the home. Other times, caregivers, embarrassed about the condition of their loved ones—or wishing to protect their dignity—remove themselves from the public eye.

> *Yea, though I walk through the valley of the shadow of death, I will fear no evil; for Thou art with me.*
>
> *Psalm 23:4 KJV*

There are many reasons for the isolation that caregivers feel, but the results are universally negative. Without positive human connections, everybody suffers. That's why it's important for caregivers to remain engaged in church, community, and other social networks. And, since caregivers can often feel lonely in a crowded room, it's important not only to attend but also to engage.

If you're one of those caregivers who's experienced a gradual separation from the outside world, today's the day to reengage. Make the effort to jumpstart old friendships and discover new ones. Cultivate healthy relationships and find appropriate ways to reconnect with the world. It's critical to push back against the isolation. You may feel awkward at first, so take it slowly. Try to avoid grasping the connectivity out of desperation; instead, enjoy the moment. After wandering in the desert and being parched, it is unwise to guzzle water. Rather, it should be slipped slowly to rehydrate properly. We don't need to pin all our hopes for friendship on one phone call or a single lunch. There will be more.

You have to be what you are.

Whatever you are, that's what you gotta be.

Johnny Cash

———⋄———

I'm Chevy Chase, and you're not.

Chevy Chase

———⋄———

There are three things extremely hard:

steel, a diamond, and to know one's self.

Benjamin Franklin

Chapter 18

LOSS OF IDENTITY

This above all: to thine own self be true.

William Shakespeare

Hamlet Act 1: scene 3

A caregiver's identity can become lost in the world, and in the details, of the one they care for. Eventually, the caregiver begins to speak almost exclusively in the first-person plural ("we") or in the third-person singular ("he" or "she"). In such cases, a conscious effort is required for the caregiver to speak in first person ("I"). Although understandable, this loss of identity leads to many problems, including codependency, resentment, depression, and the inability to make independent (and critical) decisions.

Since other folks usually focus on the person in the wheelchair, the hurting caregiver may feel ignored. And on those infrequent occasions when someone *does* inquire about the caregiver's emotional state, the caregiver may have a difficult time answering the question.

The flip-side of identity-loss is "over-sharing." Some caregivers have been so deprived of attention and interaction that their neediness gets the better of them. So, they make people "drink from the fire hose" by dousing listeners with way too much information. Given that a truckload of emotions may tumble out to the first sincere person who asks, it's usually a good idea to breathe slowly while thinking about each word.

If you're a caregiver who finds it hard to speak in the first person, it's time to reclaim your identity. Using the "I-word" may feel awkward at first, even stress-inducing. But please don't give up. Sharing from the heart takes practice and trust, but you're worth it.

I promise.

—◆—

When a codependent dies,
someone else's life flashes in front of their eyes.

—

Unknown

—◆—

PART III

—✦—

LIFESTYLE

Thou wilt show me the path of life . . . .

Psalm 16:11 KJV

Life is like a game of cards.
The hand that is dealt you represents determinism;
the way you play it is free will.

Jawaharlal Nehru

Now that my life is so prearranged
I know that it's time for a cool change.

The Little River Band, Glenn Shorrock

* · *

Happy is he who makes daily progress and
who considers not what he did yesterday
but what advance he can make today.

St. Jerome

* · *

*Greater love has no one than this,
than to lay down one's life for his friends.*

John 15:13 NKJV

Chapter 19

SUSTAINABILITY

You may have to fight a battle
more than once to win it.

Margaret Thatcher

I'm frequently asked by non-caregivers "How do I help them . . . they seem so capable." It's often hard to know what it looks like to help a high-functioning "multi-tasker" who seems capable of managing chaos, but don't be intimidated by their skill sets. Those abilities come from years of practice and repetitive behavior.

When I sit down at the piano, it looks like my fingers have a life of their own, but in reality listeners hear the culmination of decades of practice and instruction. Caregivers repeat many of the same tasks over and over, while simultaneously learning from a teacher far more demanding than even the strictest of my piano professors—fear.

Fear drives the desire we caregivers feel to wield control in an uncontrollable situation. When the wheels seem to be coming off, many of us panic and attempt to be superhuman. When presiding over a loved one's decline and suffering, it won't be tidy, and it may not get better. Yet how many of us recklessly hurl ourselves at a set of circumstances without regards to insuring sustainability?

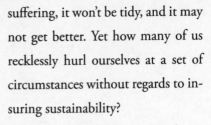

It's not that
I'm so smart;
it's just that I stay
with problems longer.

Albert Einstein

Simply because our loved one is sick or disabled doesn't guarantee we will outlive them. Yet how many caregivers structure their lives in that manner? Think of all the caregivers not seeing their own doctor regularly (72% are reported as failing to maintain regular visits with their personal physician). Think of all the caregivers who don't have life insurance. Think of all the caregivers who jeopardize their jobs by not having adequate communication with supervisors and a healthy professional plan. The list goes on of caregivers who fail to "put their mask on first."

Decades ago, I learned how to be a patient advocate with doctors, hospitals, and insurance companies—a skill that is not as complicated as one might think. Advocacy, however, is only one component of serving as a caregiver. When the crisis *du jour* of caring for a vulnerable loved one hits, I daily remind myself (and ask others to remind me) to "put my mask on first." Fear and panic never seem to take a holiday, so the battle is not in negotiating with America's health care system; it's in navigating the complex landmines of fear that lie in the heart.

The vast caregiving community is filled with people from all walks of life. Because you're reading this book, you're probably a member of that community, perhaps a longstanding member. If so, you already know the demands of the job you've taken on. You know the rewards and the pain; you know the exhilaration and the exhaustion, the isolation and the loneliness.

Throughout this book, I'll encourage you to practice *sustainable* caregiving. I'll ask you to think long and hard about the Delta Doctrine. And I'll try my best to persuade you that, if I can do it, so can you.

With the help of others who walk this journey, you and I can face that fear and make those tough unilateral decisions with the confidence that we care for our loved ones best—when we are doing so from a healthy, calm, and sustainable place.

Ask not what you can do for your country.
Ask what's for lunch.

Orson Welles

⸻ ◦►◦◄◦ ⸻

Attention to one's life-style, especially in the direction
of reducing emotional tensions, a modest but
regular program of daily exercise, a diet low in salt
and sugar and reasonably free of fatty meats and fried foods,
and plenty of good drinking water—
all these are useful and indeed essential.

Norman Cousins

⸻ ◦►◦◄◦ ⸻

Eat to live, and not live to eat.

Ben Franklin

Chapter 20

DIET

"I got so big, I had to put on my belt with a boomerang."

"I got so big, I got a shoe shine,
and had to take the man's word for it."

"I got so big, my nickname became: DAANNNNGG!"

It's certainly acceptable to stop for fast food or grab
something on the fly when a loved one is at the hospital or
having a crisis. Caregivers, however, often deal with lengthy
hospital stays and daily crises. Eventually, fast food becomes
a problem, and our bodies cry out for healthy sustenance. As
caregivers, we know what's good and not good to eat, so there's
no need to offer a diet plan, particularly when our world is
full of those. Let's instead look at this topic philosophically.

As caregivers, we feel unsettled when we don't feel in control. That unsettledness screams for comfort, and food is just a refrigerator away. To make matters worse, we're tired. And cooking is work. Weariness and stress are quickly abated by high-fat, high-calorie food. Raw broccoli just can't compare to a pastrami on rye.

Given that we are playing for inches and not miles, we shouldn't feel the need to lease out the backyard to the farmer's market and go overboard. We should, instead, take small, manageable steps toward a more healthy diet.

Grab a bottle of water, not soda. At the grocery store, pick up a bag of apples instead of those fat-laden snacks. Even a few small choices in purchasing and preparing food can result in positive results.

Make a small choice today to eat something healthy instead of something comforting. Tomorrow, do it again, and make one additional healthy choice. Before you know it, you will have trained your body, and in doing so you will have improved your emotions, your lifestyle, and your overall state of mind.

———

All you need is love.

But a little chocolate now and then doesn't hurt.

—

Charles M. Schulz

———

The best heath care combines self-care
with professional advice.

Tom Ferguson, M.D.

———◦———

I told my psychiatrist that everyone hates me.
He said I was being ridiculous—everyone hasn't met me yet.

Rodney Dangerfield

———◦———

"Ask, and God will give to you.
Search, and you will find.
Knock, and the door will open for you.
Yes, everyone who asks will receive.
Everyone who searches will find.
And everyone who knocks will have the door opened."

Matthew 7:7–8 NCV

Chapter 21

COUNSELING HELPS

Where there is no guidance, a people falls,
but in an abundance of counselors there is safety.

Proverbs 11:14 ESV

To help them sort through some of the craziness, caregivers need a trained professional, whether a psychiatrist, psychologist, social worker, or other certified mental health counselor.

Referrals can come from a variety of sources, including family physicians and pastors, and many workplaces have an Employee Assistance Program (EAP). Visits through the EAP are often limited to a half-dozen. After that, a transition plan coalesces, and further counseling becomes the employee's responsibility. I've taken advantage of those services and heartily recommend it to others. Insurance may or may not pay for visits to counselors. One visit a month, however, is well worth the cost. (Keep your receipts for tax purposes.)

Since caregivers rarely deal with short-term issues, long-term counseling is strongly advisable. Licensed clinical social workers (I like to call them the "work horses of the counseling industry") offer a tremendous source of help at affordable fees.

Counseling is an area where churches often excel. Pastors can be a great resource for caregivers, but in most cases, pastors are not able to provide continuing care. Most clergy members are well acquainted with qualified counselors and can probably refer to and transition the long-term counseling needs.

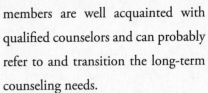

I always say shopping is cheaper than a psychiatrist.

Tammy Fay Bakker

Sometimes, a church benevolence committee will underwrite a counselor's fees, especially if church members know that their contribution will provide tangible and immediate help to someone who is dealing with an intractable situation. But even if the church can't provide long-term counseling services, the best strategy for most caregivers is straightforward: find a trained mental health professional and figure out the most practical way to engage the counselor on a regular basis. It's a sensible way to ensure that you're caring for yourself first, so that you can best care for your loved one.

If you attend a religious group that advises against counseling, you might want to rethink your participation with such a group. Pastors and other religious leaders who preach against counseling probably haven't walked through enough heartache of this kind and speak out of ignorance, so give them a wide berth.

A guy goes to the psychiatrist and says,
"Doc, I'm having the same dream every night that I'm either
a tee-pee or a wig-wam . . . what does it mean?!"
"Oh, that's easy," replied the psychiatrist.
"It just means you are too tents!"

A really old joke told to me by my father.

———— ❖ ————

I wanted you to see what real courage is,
instead of getting the idea that courage is
a man with a gun in his hand.
It's when you know you're licked before you begin,
but you begin anyway and see it through
no matter what.

Atticus Finch

Harper Lee, To Kill a Mockingbird

———— ❖ ————

If your experiences would benefit anybody,
give them to someone.

Florence Nightingale

Chapter 22

———⁂———

YOU'RE NOT ALONE: FINDING A SUPPORT GROUP

I will stand with you

When you cannot stand alone

I will fight for you

When all your strength is gone

I will sing for you

So that all can hear your song

Take my hand, lean on me, we will stand.

"We Will Stand," Peter and Gracie Rosenberger

Caregivers suffer from the three "I's": loss of **Indepen-dence**, loss of **Identity**, and **Isolation**. A support group specifically addresses the last two.

In a support group, the caregiver can interact with individuals who share the same feelings and, in many cases, share the same experiences. Support groups allow caregivers the opportunity for community and engagement at their level. The group is a safe place to share frustrations; it's also a great place to learn coping skills and pick up practical tips. In support groups, we can learn how to speak in first-person singular and share our own feelings, dreams, frustrations, heartaches, and even failures.

Support groups often meet at churches, schools, libraries, and other similar public meeting facilities. Whatever issue your loved one is going through, chances are there is a support group. From organizations such as American Cancer Society or the Alzheimer's Association to groups supporting families caring for loved ones with mental health issues, there are so many support groups available. It could be simply a general "caregiver" support group. Regardless, check a couple of them out until you find the one that connects with your circumstances . . . and then stick with it.

> Trouble shared is trouble halved.
>
> *Dorothy Sayers*

Don't look for the perfect support group; rather look for one that strengthens you and engages your heart. You're inserting yourself into a community. You may not like everyone in the group. You may not like the group. By listening and sharing, however, you are working muscles that will better equip you to stay healthy. In addition, don't underestimate how important it is for others to hear your story . . . however painful it may be. A support group engages you as an individual, provides a mechanism for you to grow as a person, and better equips you to endure. The purpose of attending support groups is not to change the issues causing us stress (which we are powerless to change), but rather to help us respond in healthier ways to the extreme challenges we face.

Let us remember therefore this lesson:
That to worship our God sincerely we must
evermore begin by hearkening to His voice,
and by giving ear to what He commands us.
For if every man goes after his own way, we shall wander.

John Calvin

⸻

Worship the LORD with gladness.
Come before him, singing with joy.
Acknowledge that the LORD is God!
He made us, and we are his.
We are his people, the sheep of his pasture.

Psalm 100:2–3 NLT

⸻

The only thing missing in Ch_rch is "u."

Seen on a Church Sign

Chapter 23

CHURCH: YOU OWE IT TO YOURSELF

I was glad when they said unto me,
Let us go into the house of the LORD.

Psalm 122:1 KJV

Attending church strengthens our faith and connects us to a loving church body. Isolation is a terrible consequence of caregiving, so connecting with a loving congregation becomes imperative.

As caregivers, attending church each time the doors are open is impossible. The goal is not to put ourselves under some type of system of rules, but rather to help set attainable and realistic targets.

Of course, you are welcome to be an atheist and deal with this stuff, but I don't recommend it. When talking to an atheist, I can't even say, "Good luck with that!" since "luck" implies something other than random chance. So, to any atheists who read this part and reject it, well, "Have at it!"

I advise avoiding "health and wealth" churches that consistently portray God as a Santa-Claus type. These churches have a "vending machine theology"—put money in; make your selection; and get what you want.

Also, I advise that you tune out church folk who tell you they know why your loved ones suffer, or try to give some sort of "consolation" prize such as, "I know what you live with is bad, but look at the good God is doing with it."

> The New Testament does not envisage solitary religion; some kind of regular assembly for worship and instruction is everywhere taken for granted in the Epistles.
>
> *C. S. Lewis*

For the record, I really don't enjoy "consolation conversations." They're just a feeble way of others trying to make sense of something that we're not going to understand this side of heaven. Gracie and I are grateful for the lives our story has touched. Every amputee who receives a limb and walks because of the organization we founded, Standing With Hope, is deeply meaningful to us. But however special those things are, they don't bring us comfort in the dark places. That comfort can only come from the knowledge that God sent His Son to rescue us from a greater tragedy than amputation, surgeries, and pain. Gracie and I both focus on that—rather than trying to wrap ourselves into theological pretzels on the "Why God" questions.

"Why doesn't God heal her?" has caused more insomnia than anything else in my life, and I have yet to rationalize an answer that makes me want to smack my forehead and say, "Ohhhh . . . that's why! I feel better now!"

Given all the hours I've logged with counselors, pastors, and with God, and considering how long I've struggled to understand earthly suffering and God's provision, I am justifiably wary of bombastic individuals who purport to know all the answers, especially if their life isn't filled with brutal challenges.

We're not going to know all the answers until we get to heaven; people who claim to have easy answers to every tragedy are best ignored. (By the way, have you noticed that people who live with great suffering tend to express more humility about "having answers"?)

To strengthen the faith and hearts of caregivers takes a community of believers who humbly minister to each other and reflect Christ into the heartache of this world. Believers who preach and model what God HAS done, versus what He might have done, equip caregivers with solid, substantial, and "grasp-worthy" faith. Such a church says, "All you need . . . is need." Such as Samuel J. Stone preaches:

> The church's one foundation is Jesus Christ her Lord;
> She is his new creation by water and the Word.
> From heaven he came and sought her to be his
> holy bride;
> with his own blood he bought her, and for her life
> he died.
>
> *"The Church's One Foundation," Samuel J. Stone*

When pastors and church leaders point the weary hearts to the Savior, they give them real hope. They walk with them, weep with them, and worship with them.

When a community of believers communicates to me that I am not alone, that God hasn't abandoned me or Gracie, and when they teach me to see the "Purpose-driven Savior," then I am strengthened.

On this side of heaven, I can't speculate on the reasons God does—or doesn't do—things that I simply cannot understand. With the love and support of a group of believers—

the church—I can, however, confidently state and rest upon what He HAS done.

Then I can, with countless others, stand and sing:

To God be the glory, great things he hath done!
So loved he the world that he gave us his Son,
who yielded his life an atonement for sin,
and opened the lifegate that all may go in.

"To God Be the Glory," Fanny Crosby

God's got this problem—He thinks He's God!

Dr. Beryl Rosenberger

━━━◆━━━

Ignorant kindness may have the effect of cruelty;
but to be angry with it as if it were direct cruelty
would be an ignorant unkindness.

George Eliot

━━━◆━━━

Mark out a straight path for your feet;
then stick to the path and stay safe.
Don't get sidetracked. . . .

Proverbs 4:26–27 NLT

Chapter 24

WHY DO FAITH HEALERS WEAR GLASSES?

We must speak where the Scripture speaks;
we must keep silent where it is silent.

John Calvin

Many people living with chronic suffering know from experience that some churches can be hazardous to your faith. Hurting individuals seeking comfort in churches may often encounter those who, when faced with affliction in others, counter it by brandishing the "Sword of the Spirit" like an axe to bludgeon those who are already badly bruised.

Admonishments such as, "If you had enough faith, Jesus would heal you," are not uncommon directives from well-meaning church folk who are poorly educated in biblical teaching; these folks suffer from a lack of understanding and compassion.

In days past, such doctrinal beliefs and behaviors remained somewhat contained to church circles. Today, however, that message blasts forth on twenty-four-hour cable, social media, and every other type of communication method (some worldwide). And, there seems to be no shortage in mass-media messages promising the next "breakthrough" to those who subscribe to a particular ministry's teachings.

Flipping channels one evening, I happened upon a broadcast of a prominent television evangelist who earned international fame by reporting miraculous healings. Ignoring the carnival-esque atmosphere of the event, my eyes immediately fixed upon the glasses perched on the preacher's nose. *Wait a minute*, I thought to myself. *Doesn't this guy believe that God will heal his poor vision?*

Do minor sufferings such as age-impacted eyesight not qualify for those who bill themselves as having an "anointing-for-healing" ministry? How much suffering is acceptable before traveling to a sawdust-floored tent to hear a man in a white suit pronounce a cure for maladies? To be fair, the tents-and-sawdust shows are now mostly a thing of the past. As the money has rolled in, the new venues-of-choice are indoor arenas with state-of-the-art sound systems and lighting.

The topic of miraculous healing continues to be a flash-point for people in and out of the church. Of course, the Bible contains many descriptions of healing, prosperity, and comfort. But, a segment of Christianity has hijacked those verses and positioned themselves as authorities on God's provision in relation to the sufferings of this world. The cartoonish behavior of some preachers often serves as fodder for comedians, but there are serious consequences. For those who suffer, the dangling carrot of healing is almost tortuous in itself.

Hurting souls often twist themselves into emotional, spiritual, and financial pretzels as they chase the rainbow of relief. Because they are desperate for healing, sufferers may believe that donating money to a particular ministry is a small price to pay for the alluring offer of God's miraculous provisions. As recently as last week, I heard one well-known minister proclaim on national television that viewers should contribute to his organization because, "God can't work a miracle on our behalf unless we act on faith."

Is that how God works? Is that how the King of kings and Lord of lords ministers to His followers? Should we offer an earnest prayer before plopping down "seed faith" or scratching a Powerball ticket?

When someone we love suffers, we try to help in any way possible. Four friends of a paralytic tore up a roof in order to lower a man down to Jesus while He preached in a crowded house. Since God created us in His own image, would reason not dictate that He feels compassion on an even greater scale than we do?

There is no question that suffering matters to God. How could it not? The Bible gives many examples of the human condition moving God's heart. The Cross stands alone as God's complete and total response to the broken estate of humanity. Furthermore, Scripture teaches that we should continually pray for those afflicted. Clearly, God would not place such directives if He planned to ignore the requests.

Yet it often seems as if our Father remains silent during agonizing days, months, years, or in my family's case—decades. My heart breaks for those who flock to individuals who preach a "rescue you from bad situations" message. I understand the appeal, and I have struggled with the desperation that drives someone to a "miracle crusade." Without any embarrassment, I admit dragging Gracie to a few of those miracle services. Walk a mile in her prosthetic legs before offering criticism.

Living with desperation for this long, however, the panic of finding a solution starts to become tedious. One can only wait for a rescue for so long, before realizing that a life must be lived, even in dire circumstances.

After decades of serving as a "wanna-be-roof-demolisher," I have also heard every type of sales pitch from those who promise relief, while failing to see the glaring inconsistency—sometimes perched upon their noses.

God does heal. I state that on faith, after almost three decades as a caregiver—while daily watching Gracie's struggles. I also remain convinced that the resurrection of Christ from the dead trumps any and all miracles. That one event indicates a power sufficient to deal with amputation, pain, and any other calamity. Remaining the bedrock of my faith and conviction, the Cross and the Resurrection continue to place all of the heartache, sadness, despair, and grief into perspective. That conviction is why I feel so passionately about encouraging others to plant themselves in a good church home. And I encourage folks to steer clear of poorly informed folks whose proclamations and advice do more harm than good.

Our strength, our faith, our human connections, and our general well-being improve by attending church. But we must also learn how to respond to those who opine regarding our loved one's condition. Don't feel the need to correct people who consider themselves "instant experts" on the suffering your loved one endures. They don't know better; it's their problem not yours. If, however, your pastor is the one making you feel uncomfortable, find another church.

You're not obligated to listen to ridiculous statements or preposterous propositions, even if those proclamations are made by self-promoters or their acolytes who quote the Bible. In Matthew 7:15, we are warned, "Beware of false prophets, who come to you in sheep's clothing but inwardly are ravenous wolves" (ESV). I don't have to go to every fight I get a ticket to; neither do you. Trying to explain sense to nonsense is simply not worth it. We can walk away, even while pushing our loved one's wheelchair, without feeling rejected by God, without the need to correct others, and without feeling guilty.

———

There is but one good; that is God.
Everything else is good when it looks to Him
and bad when it turns from Him.

—

C. S. Lewis

———

Nobody ever outgrows Scripture;
the book widens and deepens with our years.

C. H. Spurgeon

The Holy Scriptures are our letters from home.

St. Augustine

---

*"Man shall not live by bread alone,
but by every word that proceeds from the mouth of God."*

Matthew 4:4 NKJV

Chapter 25

THY WORD IS A LAMP UNTO MY FEET

Every word of God proves true;
he is a shield to those who take refuge in him.

Proverbs 30:5 ESV

The Bible doesn't lay out every answer to every question, nor does it cover every tragic scenario. What it does do, however, is clearly describe in great detail a sovereign, all-wise, loving God who bore the entire stench and judgment of man's sin upon His own Son. That same God weaves HIS purpose into even the most horrific circumstances, and one day we will see it made plain before us. When we do, every knee will bow and every tongue confess that Jesus Christ is Lord.

That knowledge has sustained uncounted millions through brutal realities and can sustain caregivers, as well.

Given that, churches are still filled with broken people, and even the best of churches will have dysfunction. A flawed church doesn't excuse our absence, but caregivers (and others) would benefit from using great wisdom when selecting a church. I make it a rule to avoid church folks who do the following:

- Talk a lot about "getting something from God," instead of focusing on what we've already received.
- Seem to have an answer for everything, which usually involves "something you have to do better."
- Spend more time talking about "getting your breakthrough" rather than focusing on the need for repentance, and trusting God's provision—even in suffering.
- Preach sermons that would make better self-help speeches. I like motivational seminars as much as the next guy, but sermons need to preach the gospel, the plan of salvation, and point to Christ.

Motivational messages don't hold up in the long run. The Gospel, however, sustains through all the pain and hardship the world can dish out. Rather than hopping around to find someone to give us the next "feel-good" and motivational-evangelical gimmick, we seek out companionship and fellowship—and develop relationships that build us up with sustainable truth.

God's plan and purpose in all of this is greater than our understanding. We are caregivers, not consultants. Focusing on what God DID do that we CAN understand, however, helps strengthen our faith and bolster courage. I know that one day I'll be in heaven with Him . . . and all of my questions will be answered. In the meantime, I choose to hang on to what Paul said in his epistle to the Romans:

> *And we know that all things work together for good to those who love God to those who are called according to His purpose.*
>
> *Romans 8:28 NKJV*

God has given us the Bible for the purpose of knowing His promises, His power, His commandments, His wisdom, His love, and His Son. As we study God's teachings and apply them to our lives, we live by the Word that shall never pass away.

Hearty laughter is a good way to jog internally
without having to go outdoors.

Norman Cousins

———— ⊷◆⊶ ————

Laughter is the sun that drives winter
from the human face.

Victor Hugo

———— ⊷◆⊶ ————

I met the surgeon general.
He offered me a cigarette.

Rodney Dangerfield

———— ⊷◆⊶ ————

Laughter gives us distance.
It allows us to step back from an event,
deal with it, and then move on.

Bob Newhart

Chapter 26

———◆◆◆———

LAUGH WHEN YOU CAN

Laughter is like a pressure valve for hurting hearts.

Jeff Foxworthy

Jeff Foxworthy and I came up with a video clip for AARP. It was called, "You Might Be a Caregiver If . . ." Here are a few highlights:

Peter: "If you have ever changed a dressing while cooking turkey and dressing, you might be a caregiver."

Jeff: "If you have ever hooked up your dog to your wife's wheelchair, just to see if it would work . . . you might be a caregiver."

Peter: "If you've ever used Neosporin as a verb, you're probably a caregiver."

Jeff: "Do it …"

Peter: "Hold still, baby, I gotta Neosporin this so we can get to church on time."

Jeff: "If anyone has ever seriously asked you, 'Baby, have you seen my left leg?'"

Peter: (Doubled over laughing and can't speak!).

———

Although humor sometimes serves as a bit of a shield to stave off painful feelings, genuinely funny moments in even the direst of circumstances continue to surprise (and delight) me.

I once heard a story about a beloved church leader from a small, rural congregation who passed away following a long illness. As a tribute and gift to the widow, the music minister offered to enlist the choir to sing the man's favorite song at the funeral. Inquiring from the bereaved woman, the music minister was surprised to hear that the dearly departed's favorite song was "Jingle Bells."

Double-checking with her, she emphatically stated that his favorite song was indeed "Jingle Bells" and expressed great gratitude that the choir offered to sing her deceased husband's much-loved song at the service.

So the music minister assembled the choir, and, with sales skills rivaling the best salesman on the planet, convinced the church choir to perform "Jingle Bells" at the funeral, which took place in June.

After the eulogy, the choir stood up and belted out, "Dashing through the snow, in a one-horse open sleigh . . ."

As the assembled crowd of family and friends looked on with puzzlement, while dressed in summer attire, the embarrassed, but committed, choir sat down feeling as if they did the best they could for the grieving widow.

At the graveside, the music minister passed by the man's wife, took her hand, and once again gave his sincere condolences. Tearfully thanking him for the music, she quizzically looked at the music minister and remarked, "I loved all the hymns and songs, but why did you all sing 'Jingle Bells'?

Wide-eyed, the music minister replied, "You stated it was his favorite song."

With a sad, but sweet, grin she put her hand to her mouth and laughed. "Ohhhh, I am so sorry. I meant, 'Golden Bells'!"

———◦◦◦———

Sometimes humor meets tragedy in strange places. Our challenge is to expect and enjoy it.

Over the years I've met quite a few comedians, and each of them makes a living seeing often painful issues through "funny-shaped" lenses. As a writer, I try to incorporate as much humor and wit as possible in all I write. People often ask me who inspires me as a writer. I usually enthusiastically state, "Lewis!" With admiration and raised eyebrows, many cerebral types respond, "C. S.?"

"No . . . Grizzard!"

In certain circles, my reply usually results in confused or disappointed faces, but I discovered two kinds of people: those who like Lewis Grizzard and those who don't know any better.

———◦◦◦———

With a vast spectrum of comedic tastes to choose from, pick one that makes your sides split. Seinfeld to Foxworthy, Andy Griffith to Tim Allen; a host of comedians compete for our amusement, so let's take them up on it! Watch a funny movie, catch a stand-up comedian on television, or read a hilarious author. When you do, you'll feel the stress melt off your heart.

Caregiving is serious business, but life can be whimsical; go with it and lighten up a bit.

———※———

If you ever start feeling like you have the goofiest, craziest,
most dysfunctional family in the world,
all you have to do is go to a state fair.
Because five minutes at the fair, you'll be going,
"You know, we're alright.
We are dang near royalty."

Jeff Foxworthy

People who cannot find time for recreation
are obliged sooner or later to find time for illness.

John Wannamaker

———◦———

A happy heart makes the face cheerful,
but heartache crushes the spirit.

Proverbs 15:13 NIV

Chapter 27

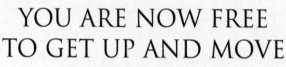

YOU ARE NOW FREE TO GET UP AND MOVE AROUND . . .

Lighten up while you still can; don't even try to understand.

Just find a place to make your stand and take it easy.

The Eagles, Glenn Frey/Jackson Browne

L ighten up. Have some fun. Take a well-deserved break. You'll be doing yourself *and* your loved one a favor.

Sometimes it is possible to have fun with the person you are caring for, but most of the time, even the "fun things" become work for caregivers who have to help their loved ones have fun.

I don't need over-the-top entertainment. I'm pretty good with a Louis L'Amour western, and, truthfully, of all the caregivers I've met in my life, 100% of them just want a quiet, restful place to be alone with their thoughts without having to worry about someone else.

When I get a break, I feel time slows down for me. Although I'm on the road a lot, I don't mind the travel, especially when I'm not taking care of another person. The TSA seems nicer, airplane food (what little there is nowadays) tastes better, the sunsets are prettier, the birds sing more, and the list goes on. It's not that I am happier per se. It's that I slow down and enjoy the little things and the quiet moments.

The abilities and stability of caregivers increase with regular rest and leisure. Even God took a Sabbath rest. Free time means just that: *free* time. We must relax and improve our state of mind and body. Wrapping our entire beings into our role as caregivers taxes the love we have for our charges and saps our identity, our creativity, and our ability to focus.

When you slow down long enough to make time for life's simple pleasures, everybody wins. So, what are you waiting for?

———⊳•⊲———

Adapt yourself to the things among which
your lot has been cast and love sincerely
the fellow creatures with whom destiny has
ordained that you shall live.

—

Marcus Aurelius

———⊳•⊲———

Through humor, you can soften
some of the worst blows that life delivers.
And once you find laughter, no matter how painful
your situation might be, you can survive it.

Bill Cosby

———◆———

First pay attention to me, and then relax.
Now you can take it easy—you're in good hands.

Proverbs 1:33 MSG

Chapter 28

LEAVE

You deserve a break today. So get up and get away . . .

Advertising Slogan for McDonald's

Honestly, we have to get some space. It doesn't have to be at McDonald's necessarily, but we caregivers need to get away on a regular basis.

For the first forty surgeries Gracie endured under my watch, I used to stay nearly around the clock with her at the hospital.

Big mistake.

Before we married, Gracie underwent her twenty-first surgery, but it was the first one with me. Although newly engaged, I had not yet "gotten my feet wet" as a caregiver, and several family members watched me to see how I would handle the pressure. The surgeon met with the family following the procedure and assured everyone that she was fine but would be in recovery for some time. Breathing a sigh of relief, we all smiled at each other, until I did the unthinkable: I went to a movie to blow off some steam and relax.

I later learned of the gasps and disapproval by some of the women gathered around. One of them was the mother-in-law of one of my relatives, and had no "skin in the game," but she felt it her duty to properly evaluate my behavior and hold up a scorecard as if she served as an Olympic judge during a diving contest.

It didn't help that she was also a "holier than thou" type. You know the ones: They have a bumper sticker on their Cadillac that states "My Other Car Is a Chariot of Fire!"

While I took a break and enjoyed myself at the movie, the judgment piled higher, as the group seemed to revel in how I "just wasn't up to the task."

A friend pulled me aside to share all this with me, and I mistakenly acted contrite to get into good graces with everyone. My instincts, however, were exactly right. Gracie had a whole team of nurses and doctors *at the hospital*. She needed me *after* those professionals were no longer available.

For a one-time event like a broken arm or something, this "get-away" principle doesn't necessarily apply. Issues stretching over years, however, are "game changers."

So, when help is present, take advantage of it by leaving the premises and allowing fresh air into your body and soul. Caregivers require regular breaks, preferably without being criticized by others.

While I'm at it, I developed a policy about people who criticize how I handle caregiving issues and the decisions I make as a caregiver: *The length of time I will listen to someone criticize is in direct proportion to how much time the critic spends helping.*

If you like that policy, you are welcome to use it, and I hope it helps stave off those who simply want to gripe.

————⊰◈⊱————

When managing your lifestyle, the three "L's" become an easy tool to remind yourself to take it easy: "LAUGH, LEISURE, LEAVE." So, here's a **1-2-30 reminder.**

1: Do at least one special thing for yourself each week.

Catch a movie, golf, go to a museum, ride your bike, go fishing, or find something else you enjoy. Do one special something for yourself every week. Sometimes I like catching a movie or a good book, but other times I find myself alone in the sanctuary at our church playing the piano for an hour or two.

If you need someone to sit with your loved one while you take a break, call your church. If your church won't help with that, ask a friend (and then change churches).

2: Take at least two weeks' annual vacation from caregiving each year.

You probably can't take fourteen days off in a row, but by spreading it over the year, it becomes possible. It's roughly a day and a night off every month. Yes, it may mean asking for help from others. That's where the church offers great assistance.

Church leaders can help find a person who can help, or even find the funds to pay for skilled care of some type (RN, LPN), or work with a local caregiver respite organization to provide someone to stay overnight while you get out of town for a night or so.

Most services that offer something like that run around $15–20 per hour (depending upon location). Although that sounds like a lot of money, there are ways around the costs.

The challenge for caregivers is to make the commitment to care for themselves, and then watch the resources appear. Experience teaches me that it's not a lack of resources but a lack of resourcefulness that prohibits progress.

Churches are full of professionals, students, young people, retired members, and so forth, who can volunteer. Most caregivers have some sort of family structure to help share the load, but for those who do not, a church family becomes imperative. It is important for the church to bring its considerable resources to the table by helping with extreme caregiver situations, such as single mothers with a special needs child, elderly spouses caring for each other, one person dealing with a catastrophic illness over lengthy periods of time, etc.

It's not enough to simply write a check. The goal is sustainability for the caregiver—and that often means developing a professional plan, as well. Churches are equipped with business and community leaders who can provide that type of counsel to those single parents/young families with special needs children or those at middle-age struggling to balance work with caregiving. Avoid sending a check; instead, develop a plan.

30: Take at least thirty minutes a day to enjoy
something humorous.

Television is full of sitcoms (some of them stupid; others profane and disgusting), but somewhere in all of that programming, there are laughs waiting for you. Go get them. If television is not your thing, load comics onto your iPod and listen to them while going for a walk, and kill two birds with one stone (or, like Chuck Norris, you can kill two stones with one bird!).

For the frugal, your local library has all kinds of things just waiting for you to check them out! Find something that makes you laugh for thirty minutes a day! I download to my phone a free app of jokes that just make me cry with laughter. Granted, amusing me is not difficult, but the benefit is a better disposition and a little lighter outlook. Everyone has a sense of humor, but caregivers may require a bit more help cultivating theirs.

Caregiving is hard, wearisome work—you deserve an occasional break from the daily grind. With these few ideas, you can inject a lot of sunshine and fresh air into a dreary situation. By doing so, the one you love benefits from a healthy caregiver—and you as the caregiver give yourself permission to live a more meaningful and joyful life.

—◦—

Laughter is to life what
shock absorbers are to automobiles.
It won't take the potholes out of the road,
but it sure makes the ride smoother.

—

Barbara Johnson

—◦—

You can easily judge the character of a man by
how he treats those who can do nothing for him.

Johann Wolfgang von Goethe

———◆———

There never was any heart truly great and generous,
that was not also tender and compassionate.

Robert Frost

Chapter 29

<hr />

SEPARATE THE PERSON FROM THE PAIN

Beyond all these things put on love,
which is the perfect bond of unity.

Colossians 3:14 NASB

How do you keep love and passion thriving in a chronic medical catastrophe where the suffering is not limited to a short-term illness or injury?

Different from Alzheimer's or dementia, couples impacted by one spouse's living with a broken or diseased body while retaining complete cognitive awareness presents a different set of emotional trials for the marriage. The challenge for the healthy spouse is to maneuver through the minefield of medical issues, attending to each of them, but never losing sight of the suffering person's heart. Taking care of the body does not always equate to caring for the heart.

The challenge for the sick or injured spouse, even from a wheelchair—or while experiencing severe chronic pain—is to recognize that matters of the heart, though often less demanding, are just as important (if not more so) as the needs of the body.

If your loved one is suffering from a life-altering condition, it's imperative that you separate the person from the pain. Doing so is difficult but not impossible. With lots of practice, plenty of prayer, help from those who will give it, and consistent encouragement from trusted counselors, you'll keep reminding yourself that the person you're caring for is much more than a name on a chart.

> If I'm laden at all
> I'm laden with sadness
> That everyone's heart
> Isn't filled with the gladness
> Of love for one another.
>
> *"He Ain't Heavy, He's My Brother"*
> *Bobby Scott and Bob Russell*

Son, daughter, parent, spouse, sibling, cousin, friend—a person, not a patient. Their challenges *belong* to them but are *not* them. Although my wife is missing both legs, she is defined by so much more than the sum or lack of body parts. By looking beyond disabilities and deformities, we release ourselves from a previously unknown bondage of judging others by a faulty standard of normal.

That newfound freedom enables us to love with precision—right to the heart. In doing so, we discover priceless moments of joy in the relationship, even if they can't respond to us in a way that we desire. Recognizing the inexhaustible source of love flowing from God frees us to unreservedly pour love into others.

A man who gives in to temptation after
five minutes simply does not know
what it would have been like an hour later.

C. S. Lewis

———◆———

The grace of God is the one thing we cannot do
without in this life or in the life to come;
it has no substitutes, artificial, temporary, or otherwise.

Bill Bright

———◆———

You lay your bets and then you pay the price
The things we do for love, the things we do for love.

"The Things We Do for Love," 10 CC

Graham Gouldman/Eric Stewart

Chapter 30

WHEN EMOTIONS TURN
SELF-DESTRUCTIVE

Be sober, be vigilant; because your adversary the devil walks
about like a roaring lion, seeking whom he may devour.

1 Peter 5:8 NKJV

Over-stressed caregivers may convince themselves that they've earned the right to "blow off a little steam." I know. I've been there, thought that, done that, and got the scars to prove it.

I had to learn the hard way that strong emotions, combined with unrelenting stress and sheer exhaustion, make a dangerous mix.

Here in the twenty-first century, temptations are completely and thoroughly woven into the fabric of everyday life. So, unless you're a hermit living on a deserted island without

WiFi, you'll probably be tempted by somebody or something *today*—in fact, you will probably be tempted on countless occasions. Why? Because you live in a world that's filled to the brim with temptations and addictions that can lead you far, far away from your family, your faith, your personal responsibilities, and your Maker.

Like the old saying goes, "The price of freedom is eternal vigilance." If you're always vigilant, you can stay out of the trap; if you let down your guard, you may get snared.

Caregivers can't effectively live and serve others if they're carrying around massive loads of guilt and shame. So what are we, as mere mortals, to do when we fall short? The answer, in my opinion, is summed up in a five-letter word: G-R-A-C-E.

By constantly reminding ourselves that God's grace covers our sins (not so we have a license to keep repeating them), we discover that guilt no longer whips us into a frenzy. Grace frees us to love and to serve from a clean heart.

From experience I know the agony of trying to serve as a caregiver while maintaining a life filled with destructive coping mechanisms. To be clear, the challenges of caregiving don't cause character defects, they only amplify them—and can act like "Miracle Grow" for our faults. When those faults lead caregivers to cope using sex, alcohol, drugs, or other addictions, these harmful "escapes" always lead down a destructive path.

We live in a fallen, broken world where bad things happen, often without a fairy-tale ending. That won't change until Christ returns. And, if you want to navigate your way safely through that fallen world, you'll guard yourself against the misplaced emotions and the self-destructive behaviors that are tearing our families and our society apart.

You can't be perfect. But there are several things you *can* do. Seeing a counselor once a month and support groups twice a month, calling a close friend or pastor regularly that you can trust with your weakness and weariness; these are ways that you can push back against temptations.

Whatever "relief" that's "promised" by various coping mechanisms—such as illicit sexual activity, illicit emotional activity, drugs, or alcohol—is a lie that will rip you apart.

You don't have to take my word for it; you're certainly free to chart your own path.

But as someone who's made virtually every mistake one can make on this journey, I don't recommend it. I've found it wise to listen to people with a lot of scars. Their experience can help me avoid the injuries they've endured.

Life is not always what one wants it to be,
but to make the best of it, as it is,
is the only way of being happy.

Jenny Jerome Churchill

———◦———

We deem those happy who, from the experience of life,
have learned to bear its ills,
without being overcome by them.

Juvenal

———◦———

There are two ways of meeting difficulties:
You alter the difficulties, or you alter yourself to meet them.

Phyllis Bottome

Chapter 31

KEEP LIVING,
EVEN WHILE HURTING

Live the life you are given as well as you can.

Cardinal Joseph Bernadine

It is appropriate to acknowledge our hurts. But, after nearly three decades of living with someone who daily suffers from severe chronic pain, I have witnessed the difference between "living with pain" versus "living while in pain." My wife didn't have to go to Africa and launch a prosthetic limb ministry. She could have easily chosen to focus on herself and her own challenges. She purposed, however, to give out of her lack—and in doing so, she continues to touch a great many lives even though she can no longer travel. She saw something worthwhile that did not reduce her pain but rather transcended it. The lesson I learned from her is:

it's possible and rewarding to live a full and rich life while in pain.

We don't have to wait until we "feel good" before we participate in life. And, we don't have to wait until we're "healthy" before we succeed. I remember a special night in Madison Square Garden right after President George W. Bush gave his acceptance speech for the nomination in 2004. Invited to be on the platform behind the President following Gracie's performance at the convention two nights prior, we had to be in place on the stage early in the evening. For several hours we sat there, while my wife's pain levels escalated. She knew she would be uncomfortable, and she knew it would be a long night, but we lived in the moment together, and after the President left, we danced together among the fallen balloons and confetti while country singer Lee Ann Womack stood just feet away singing her hit song, "I Hope You Dance."

Gracie did opt to forgo wearing dress shoes in order to be a bit more comfortable. You can still see us in pictures sitting just behind the President's left shoulder. Gracie's robotic-looking legs are in plain view with her bright white sneakers, which I think is hilarious! If Gracie and the President of the United States didn't mind, no one else should!

If we wait until we feel good or until things are "going our way" before we choose to engage in life, we are missing out on undiscovered joy and deeply rewarding moments—we're missing out on life.

We're as miserable or happy as we choose to be.

And when you get the choice to sit it out or dance.

I hope you dance.

"I Hope You Dance"

Mark D. Sanders/Tia Sillers

PART IV

❦

PLANNING

The plans of the diligent lead surely to plenty.

Proverbs 21:5 NKJV

A danger foreseen is half avoided.

Thomas Fuller

Life is about not knowing, having to change,
taking the moment and making the best of it,
without knowing what's going to happen next.

Gilda Radner

———◆———

Crisis brings us face to face with our inadequacy
and our inadequacy in turn leads us
to the inexhaustible sufficiency of God.

Catherine Marshall

Chapter 32

CRISIS MANAGEMENT IS AN OXYMORON

There cannot be a crisis next week.

My schedule is already full.

Henry Kissinger

Caregiving not only affects the caregiver's health and emotions but also their lifestyle.

- 20 hours per week is the average number of hours family caregivers spend attending to their loved ones.
- 13% of family caregivers are providing 40 hours of care a week or more.

With responsibilities like these, you can forget trying to plan a vacation; it's usually a major event just to go to see a movie!

Starting out each morning anticipating the "crisis du jour," we caregivers frequently throw our hands up in exasperation at trying to schedule and reschedule things. With the daily bombardment of medical and caregiving issues, is it possible to carve out some things to improve our overall well-being? It doesn't require a trip to Italy or an exotic island beach. Is it too much to ask for a quiet cot in the corner with no one bothering us for a couple of hours?!

In the context of caregiving, feeling better about ourselves is not a selfish and egocentric pursuit. A more relaxed, self-confident, and emotionally calm caregiver almost guarantees that his/her charge will receive better and more consistent care. If the loved one is not cognitively impaired, the relationship can even deepen when a caregiver feels rested and refreshed.

I can't give you precise solutions to the crises you'll face. But what I can promise you is the following:

- Every crisis will eventually pass.
- You'll be better equipped to weather the crisis if you've already created a support system that includes a church, a counselor, and a support group.

- You'll be better equipped to face tomorrow's crisis if you take care of yourself today.

Every caregiver needs time off, but fear, obligation, and guilt (FOG) often shelve breaks. Getting away is not easy, and it may have to be in small but consistent chunks of time. Carving out "downtime" is paramount to serving as a good caregiver. I know your loved one suffers—so does mine—but you and I can't change that fact, nor will we help them by driving ourselves until we're nothing but a husk.

Nothing in the world can take the place of persistence.
Talent will not; genius will not; education will not.
Persistence and determination alone are omnipotent.

Calvin Coolidge

———◆———

I walk slowly, but I never walk backwards.

Abraham Lincoln

———◆———

About all I ever did was stick with it.

Bear Bryant

———◆———

This is the day the LORD has made;
we will rejoice and be glad in it.

Psalm 118:24 NKJV

———◆———

Make each day your masterpiece.

John Wooden

Chapter 33

CAREGIVING,
ONE DAY AT A TIME

The most important history is the history we make today.

Henry Ford

Caregiving is one of the toughest jobs on planet Earth. It's a job that almost nobody can do for a lifetime but anyone can do for twenty-four hours. What's required is patience, a willingness to do each day's work as it comes, and a commitment to focus on today's work, not the worries of tomorrow.

Robert Louis Stevenson could have been talking directly to caregivers when he wrote:

Anyone can carry his burden, however hard, until nightfall. Anyone can do his work, however hard, for one day. Anyone can live sweetly, patiently, lovingly, purely, till the sun goes down. And this is all that life really means.

Every day presents its own set of challenges and opportunities. Yesterday's opportunities are gone forever, and tomorrow's may never come. It's okay to look backwards but don't stare. The future is beyond my control as well. But today's opportunities are very real and, because you're a caregiver, critical to the well-being of your loved one.

Today, because you're a caregiver, you can make a positive impact on the life of another human being.

Today, because you're a caregiver, you can make your corner of the world a better place.

Today, because you're a caregiver, you can be a living, breathing example of what it means to be a true servant.

Today, you can share God's love through a smile, a hug, a kind word, or a heartfelt prayer.

Yesterday? That's over and done. It's a cancelled check.

Tomorrow? That's God's business, and He'll figure out what to do with it.

So, that leaves only a single solitary day that's available for our use. Here's how Jesus said it should be used:

—◦—

But seek first his kingdom and his righteousness,
and all these things will be given to you as well.
Therefore do not worry about tomorrow,
for tomorrow will worry about itself.
Each day has enough trouble of its own.

—

Matthew 6:33–34 NIV

—◦—

"In quietness and trust is your strength."

Isaiah 30:15 NASB

The best remedy for those who are afraid,
lonely or unhappy is to go outside, somewhere where
they can be quite alone with the heavens, nature and God.

Anne Frank

Be still, my soul: the Lord is on thy side.
Bear patiently the cross of grief or pain.
Leave to thy God to order and provide;
In every change, He faithful will remain.
Be still, my soul: thy best, thy heavenly Friend
Through thorny ways leads to a joyful end.

"Be Still My Soul," Katharina von Schlegel

I wait quietly before God, for my hope is in him.

Psalm 62:5 NLT

Chapter 34

———✦———

MAKING TIME
FOR QUIET TIME

Here's a gift you give yourself. Sometime in your day today,
try to turn off all the noises you can around you,
and give yourself some quiet time.

Fred Rogers

Here's a simple little prescription for becoming a better caregiver: carve out some quiet time every day. In our noisy, twenty-first-century world, silence is highly under-rated. Many of us can't even seem to walk from the front door to the street without a cell phone or an iPod in our ear. The world seems to grow louder day by day, and our senses seem to be invaded at every turn.

If we allow the distractions of this clamorous society to totally envelope our days, we do ourselves a profound disservice. Being still takes practice. The first time you try it, you may fall asleep. Good. Try it again the next day. Frantic people make frantic decisions. Someone in your life is counting on you to make good ones. Would you trust your well-being to someone who stays frazzled?

Rather than spending our entire days glued to our electronic devices, we're wise to carve out a few moments for quiet reflection. When we do, we are rewarded and so are the ones we care for.

Are you simply too busy to grab a few minutes of quiet time each day? If so, it's probably time to rearrange your to-do list.

As a caregiver, it's your responsibility to stay emotionally healthy. Quiet time helps you stay that way. But don't take my word for it. Just ask Mr. Rogers.

—◆—

That's why I'm easy
I'm easy like Sunday morning.

—

"Easy Like Sunday Morning"
Lionel Richie, The Commodores

—◆—

A hospital bed is a parked taxi with the meter running.

Groucho Marx

———※———

Money is a terrible master but an excellent servant.

P. T. Barnum

———※———

I have enough money to last me the rest of my life,
unless I buy something.

Jackie Mason

Chapter 35

——❦——

ADDING MONEY CHALLENGES TO THE MIX

The wise see danger ahead and avoid it. . . .

Proverbs 22:3 NCV

Caregiving is challenging enough, but adding money issues to the mix creates a massive strain on individuals and families. Three decades of caregiving experience leads me to believe that, although they may help, I cannot permanently rely on a government program, an individual, a family member, or a lottery ticket to come to my rescue. *By the way, the lottery is simply a tax on people who are bad at math.*

What I am sure of is this: Caregiving requires long hours, weary nights, and constant battles to stretch a dollar until it is translucent.

From a server struggling to make tips working at a restaurant while caring for a sick spouse, to multimillionaire children able to pay for full-time care for aging parents, I've encountered individuals in virtually every type of caregiving situation. Most of us fall somewhere in the middle, but we lean toward the server trying to squeeze out a living.

- Caregiving families (families in which one member has a disability) have median incomes that are more than 15% lower than non-caregiving families. In every state the poverty rate is higher among families with members with a disability than among families without.

- During the 2009 economic downturn, one in five family caregivers had to move into the same home with their loved ones to cut expenses.

- 47% of working caregivers indicate an increase in caregiving expenses has caused them to use up all or most of their savings.

- The average family caregiver for someone fifty years or older spent $5,531 per year on out-of-pocket caregiving expenses in 2007, which was more than 10% of the median income for a family caregiver that year.

Many financial experts share strategies for dealing with money, getting out of debt, and saving for retirement, yet I've not heard one of them who has even remotely juggled anything like my family's three decades of surgeries, pain, constant crises, and health costs (cresting $9 million). Here are a few of the dilemmas I've pondered over the years:

- What kind of financial impact will the illness have on our family's budget?
- How does this affect my ability to pay my bills, realize professional potential and earn more, prepare for retirement, have peace of mind, or tithe to my church?
- How do I keep my head above water?
- Is it possible to "get ahead"?

These questions (and many more) serve as the regular topics during my frequent late-night conversations with the ceiling fan.

Before launching my radio show and writing my book, *Wear Comfortable Shoes: Surviving and Thriving as a Caregiver*, I spent a great deal of time thinking about this: What does "help" look like to a caregiver? For example, having someone bring meals to the family is helpful, but eventually someone has to learn to cook.

Likewise with money: A gift of cash in time of need is

helpful. Ultimately, however, one must earn a living and effectively manage money.

The key is sustainability, and in order to manage the massive bills, extra costs, and nuances of the tax code, I have found that I need the help of trained professionals—specifically certified public accountants (CPA).

I look at a CPA almost like a primary care doctor. To me, the CPA functions as the "hub" of the financial wheel of life. From mortgages to tax deductions, a CPA can serve as a guide through the financial jungle of both individual budgets and our national economy. When my heating unit needs servicing, I leave it to the professionals. When my financial "unit" needs servicing, I also call the professionals.

How many accountants does it take to change a light bulb?
Hmmm . . . I'll just do a few numbers and get back to you!

How can you tell when an accountant is on vacation?
He shows up at 8:30 a.m.

The Accountant's Prayer
Lord, help me become more flexible . . .
Starting tomorrow morning at 7:59 a.m. CST

I won't presume to tell anyone, particularly caregivers, how to manage their money. I can offer another **1-2-30 reminder** that changed the way I view money, helped me keep a superior credit rating and avoid bankruptcy while dealing with the massive medical bills incurred for the last several decades.

- Find one charity that has nothing to do with your situation that you can regularly support. It may be only $5 per month, but I find it helpful to make a positive difference into someone else's life and not be consumed with my own.

- Make sure you see your financial counselor at least twice a year to ensure that budgets are met, taxes are filed, and there is some sustainable plan. Since it is inconsistent to call yourself a caregiver if you don't have life insurance, make one of those visits with a financial planner.

- Sock $30 per paycheck into some sort of savings/rainy day fund. Some can do $30,000, but most of us can't. Do what you can but try to hit at least $30 per paycheck.

You have power over your mind—not outside events.
Realize this, and you will find strength.

Marcus Aurelius, Meditations

———◆———

Not being able to govern events, I govern myself.

Michel de Montaigne

Chapter 36

ABOUT INSURANCE, DOCTORS, AND THE SYSTEM

These should learn first of all to put their religion
into practice by caring for their own family. . . .

1 Timothy 5:4 NIV

As a caregiver, you need insurance—not just medical. In fact, I maintain that you shouldn't even call yourself a caregiver if you don't have life insurance.

Life insurance is simple. You buy it, you pay the premiums, and that's that.

Health insurance, on the other hand, can be a little more tricky but certainly not as hard as some would make you think. Health care is complicated. Heath insurance, not so much. I can attest, however, that while the healthcare system is complex, it's not impossible to navigate. One quick tip; I've never heard of any property insurance company selling a policy on a car after the wreck. If you postpone getting health insurance because you're not currently sick, you're playing Russian roulette, and, quite truthfully, you're part of the problem in our country.

After countless explanations of benefits (EOB) from now seven different insurance companies covering an immense amount of procedures and medical needs, I have never lost an appeal.

From nurses to surgeons, I have confronted, managed, appealed to, and recruited more medical professionals to my viewpoint than I can recall. I treat each of them with deference but not subservience.

Each professional who cares for my wife receives a paycheck; I do not. Volunteering does not make me special, but I am different. My stake in the journey is unlike those who do it for a living. My status as a spouse also places me in a category distinct from relatives who volunteer. I remain the only person in Gracie's life not connected by blood or money who has willingly chosen to care for her in this manner.

Understanding the role and motivation of an individual better equips you to speak to the core issue and need. A child caring for a parent will have different needs than a sibling or spouse caregiver. A medical professional will also have a different sort of needs. Saying that they're just doing it for a paycheck is a cop-out. There's an underlying reason why they chose this profession. When negotiating with them, learn and speak to that reason. That's how you move the ball down the field as an advocate.

While I cannot give you a comprehensive guide to every health insurance issue, here are a few things I've learned along the way.

Be polite, but don't grovel: As you navigate through the healthcare system, angry words rarely help the situation. But neither does subservience. So don't scream and shout. But if you know you're right, stand your ground. Say what you mean, mean what you say . . . but don't say it mean.

Remember that when it comes to your loved one, you're an expert too: As I shared with one surgeon recently, "With all due respect, Doctor, I've cared for Gracie since you were in junior high school—*and I know what I'm talking about.*"

Keep good records: I know record-keeping is a pain, and I understand that it's hard to keep up with the inevitable mountains of paperwork. But it's necessary. When the time comes to make your case, you need to be fully informed not completely confused. I scan and keep them electronically, and everything is backed up. I don't have room in my office for the volume of data Gracie generates.

Don't be intimidated: The healthcare system is big, but you and your loved one still have rights. If you think your claims are valid, don't be afraid to say so loudly and often.

Dress appropriately: Face it, who would you defer to: a man in a suit with a groomed appearance or a guy in cut-offs and in a Van Halen T-shirt?

Practice speaking: Ask someone you trust to verify whether or not you butcher the Queen's English. I don't make the rules, but if you come across like a rube, people will treat you like one. Shakespeare said, "Brevity is the soul of wit." Condense your thoughts into the smallest ideas, concepts, and questions so that you get right to the heart of the issue without the drama, stammering, or wasting of time because you didn't do your due diligence. I had a prepared ninety-second speech I once gave to a doctor. I practiced it while driving, working around the house, etc. When the appointment came, I delivered. And I won.

Practice writing: It is always a good idea to write out things for each doctor visit. Go back and edit if needed.

Get a case worker: When dealing with a long-term chronic illness/disability, your medical insurance should have a case-worker they can assign to you. For many years, ours was an RN named Paul, who was simply a GREAT guy. He and I talked often and became good friends. He developed a strong grasp of Gracie's injuries and needs, provided great leadership to me, and served as a friendly liaison to the insurance company. A case worker from your loved one's medical insurance company will save you time, headache, heartache, and even money.

Care advocate: When negotiating with an insurance company, if you feel like David against Goliath, you're not alone—and don't try to do it alone. There are companies that provide patient care advocates. This service becomes hugely helpful if your loved one lives in a different town. Usually a nurse or similarly trained professional, they work for you, not the insurance company, hospital, or physician. They can fight (and win) battles that you just may be too weary or unable to engage.

What to bring to a fight: Sometimes, you will be at odds with your insurance company—it happens, but don't panic. I don't appeal to the humanity of insurance companies (it's a corporation not a person), nor do I argue with them with a Bible in one hand and the US Constitution in the other. Through math, I am able to demonstrate how it's in their best interest to cover a particular drug or procedure (make sure it is!)

To paraphrase the old saying about going to a fight, "If they bring a knife, I'll bring a calculator." Math wins every time.

⟹◆⟸

I remember sitting in the critical-care family waiting area once and noticed a man standing helplessly in the middle of the room, twisting his cap. Wearing work boots and dressed as if he stepped right off the farm, this frightened man looked completely out of his element.

Evaluating his clothing, I surmised that in his world, he was most likely extremely capable around heavy machinery, possibly livestock. In his world, he was an expert.

But he was no longer in his world. In the world he now found himself, people dressed strangely, talked in codes and different languages, moved at light speed, and days and nights often ran together. Beeping, screaming, constant pages on the intercom, unfamiliar sights and smells—think about the shock of the harsh new environment, and then add that to the worry and fear over his loved one lying in critical care.

This is the world we caregivers live in, and we must adapt. Otherwise, we will be at the mercy of that world until it chews us and our loved ones up.

In that critical area waiting room, I decided that, although I couldn't control it, I also wouldn't be at the mercy of that world.

You don't have to, either.

"But as for you, be strong and do not give up,
for your work will be rewarded."

2 Chronicles 15:7 NIV

———✦———

Do Lipton employees take coffee breaks?

Steven Wright

Chapter 37

YOUR OTHER CAREER

If I do my full duty, the rest will take care of itself.

George S. Patton

According to a 2009 study conducted by the National Alliance for Caregiving in collaboration with AARP, approximately "73% of family caregivers who care for someone over the age of eighteen either work or have worked while providing care." With 65 million Americans serving as volunteer caregivers for vulnerable loved ones, it's clear that a vast number of today's workers are saddled with the extra responsibilities of caregiving. And with baby boomers racing into senior status, tomorrow's workforce will find itself struggling to care for a huge population of aging parents.

The alarm bells are sounding: A large number of individuals will require volunteer caregivers, and the trend clearly reveals that more and more workers will need to juggle their professional lives while caring for their loved ones.

MetLife provided a 2010 study that showed American workers from every profession are struggling to balance work responsibilities while serving as caregivers. The MetLife report revealed significantly higher costs to the employer, ranging from absenteeism to health care. These costs to American businesses soar into the billions (*The MetLife Study of Working Caregivers and Employer Health Care Costs*).

In a robust economy, those costs and challenges to employers can be absorbed or accommodated somewhat easier. But in the difficult times facing many of today's businesses, caregivers must function with extra care to avoid taxing the goodwill of employers and coworkers—as well as the "bottom line."

The caregiver who daily attends to the needs of the patient serves as a critical component of that patient's overall health. Although it's difficult to quantify the exact value added by a caregiver, all can agree that a gainfully employed caregiver is in the best interest of the patient.

Paychecks, housing, insurance, food—the entire patient-care ecosystem for many individuals—depends upon the physical, emotional, and professional health of the caregiver. Certainly not all patients have a family member or friend serving as a caregiver, and clearly not all caregivers maintain full-time employment. Yet, according to the studies, millions of American workers are serving as volunteer caregivers for an aging, disabled, or chronically ill loved one.

As someone who has faced this issue on an extreme level, I receive many requests to address this topic. My passion is to equip caregivers with easy and practical tips, not only for staying employed but also for excelling in the workplace.

One of the most challenging issues I face as a caregiver for twenty-eight years is balancing work and my wife's chronic and pressing medical issues.

I recall days that began normally. But on those "normal" days, my wife had been admitted to the hospital and scheduled for surgery by the time our sons' school let out. Juggling the medical crisis alone is challenging. Living up to work responsibilities, however, while somehow keeping the plates spinning—picking up children, fixing meals, and swinging by the hospital to meet with doctors—can make for extremely stressful workdays.

When the caregiver is the business owner or boss, scheduling work may be easier, but the stress of keeping the business going brings additional challenges.

Employees serving as caregivers regularly find themselves in tight work situations that often require appeasing one demand, while disappointing another. Saying "no" to a hurting family member in order to maintain work responsibilities can significantly strain an already-stretched home life. Saying "no" to an employer, however, presents a new basket of problems. Caregivers often find themselves balancing on a professional tightrope: not abusing the generosity of fellow employees and supervisors while keeping crises on the home front at bay.

Is it any wonder that many caregivers decline promotions—and the increased wages that accompany the increased responsibilities—in order to avoid the extra duties that comes with workplace advancement? Sometimes, it is even easier to leave the workforce altogether. The caregiver's decision to retreat from the workplace has permanent effects that ripple through the family, the community, and, when multiplied many times over, the nation's economy.

For many years, I took jobs I really did not aspire to, all for insurance and flexibility of schedule. Like many caregivers, my earning potential and advancement took hits on numerous occasions. Also, like many caregivers, I learned to adapt and "figured out how to make it work." Along the journey, I discovered that although many bosses and supervisors possessed understanding, they still required good communication about the circumstances.

It was while balancing work and caregiving that I learned the three "F's."

- Be FORTHRIGHT with the boss
- Ask for FLEXIBILITY
- Give a FAIR day's work

If you're a caregiver who's juggling responsibilities at work and at home, nobody needs to tell you how tough that job can be. But from personal experience, I can tell you that, while the job is hard, it's not impossible. You can be *both* a primary caregiver *and* a valuable addition to your workplace.

It is always your next move.

Napoleon Hill

———◆———

Nothing is so exhausting as indecision,
and nothing is so futile.

Bertrand Russell

———◆———

I made up my mind, but I made it up both ways.

Casey Stengel

Chapter 38

UNILATERAL DECISIONS

The best decision-makers are those who are
willing to suffer the most over their decisions
but still retain their ability to be decisive.

M. Scott Peck

Sitting across the table from a man caring for his wife who
suffers from Parkinson's disease, I couldn't help but see
the weariness in his eyes and on his face.

When a mutual friend asked me to meet with him, the
comment was simply, "He's worn out, and I think you could
be of help to him."

"Worn out" seemed to be an understatement.

Stirring his coffee, this retired physician reflected, "I
miss playing golf with my friends."

Listening for a little while longer, I recalled what I have
come to call the three "I's" that plague every caregiver:

- The loss of INDEPENDENCE
- The ISOLATION
- The loss of IDENTITY

Immediately identifying the first two, I asked him, "Do you have the resources to hire someone part-time?" The predictable response came quickly, "She's not comfortable with having someone come into our home." Noticing the avoidance of speaking in first-person singular, I simply replied, "I didn't ask what she was comfortable doing."

The loss of identity, where the wants and needs of a loved one consumes a caregiver, remains one of the most challenging components when it comes to helping a caregiver. From such phrases as, "We just got home from the hospital . . ." or "He's having a bad day . . ." or "Our days are filled with . . ."—speaking in first-person singular all but fades away.

I understand feeling that loss of identity—perhaps on levels few will. Serving as a caregiver since age twenty-two, I've never really known any other lifestyle as an adult. Daily teetering close to the edge of collapsing emotionally, physically, and/or financially wears on a soul, and it is a challenge facing 65 million Americans caring for loved ones.

Looking at this husband in torment, I gently but firmly stated, "You're not violating your marriage by making unilateral decisions." Adding, as he lifted his eyes, "Sometimes the ones we love can't see past their fear, their illness, or their pain. As caregivers, we have to think of the good of the 'unit' not just the sick/disabled person. That means we have to make decisions that will protect the health and well-being of the caregiver—even if it means going against the wants of the person receiving care."

A person in pain, on heavy medication, suffering from dementia, or dealing with a severe disability or illness can't always see beyond their immediate need. Their cries for relief often overpower the gentle whisper of wisdom that cautions us to take a break. The guilt of making unilateral decisions, particularly for spouses and children caring for elderly parents, can be crushing.

We're mobile, they're not.
They're in pain, we're not.
They cling—we feel suffocated.

These and other dynamics play out daily (often hourly) in the relationships of caregivers and their charges. In spite of the conflicting feelings, caregivers must get fresh air and allow themselves to step back and make hard decisions for the good of the patient and themselves—and they often have to do that while feeling horribly alone and scared.

Looking across the table at the coffee shop, I saw familiar feelings cascade over my new friend's face. A smart man, a capable man, a loving husband and father, and a weary and lonely caregiver—I knew his turmoil well, and my heart broke for him. Unlike someone who is warm and well-fed trying to relate to someone who is hungry and cold, we caregivers recognize and relate to each other because we live it.

I asked him point-blank, "How would you like to resume your Tuesday golf outings with your buddies, have lunch at the club, play another round in the afternoon—and then come home to find your wife bathed, dressed, the house clean, and dinner prepared?"

As the tears filled his eyes, he simply said, "I can't imagine how wonderful that would be."

"You are one phone call away from prying your hands off the wheelchair and putting them on the golf club—make the call."

To his credit, he phoned the service I recommended, and they worked a wonderful schedule of help coming to the house. His problem was not financial—it was guilt and conflicting emotions.

The best way to help a caregiver is to see and acknowledge the internal conflict those feelings create—and gently walk them through learning to make better choices to not only help themselves, but ultimately help those they are giving treasure, sweat, and even blood to help. The one we care for won't be helped by depleting ourselves emotionally, physically, and financially.

A reporter once asked me, "WWJD (What would Jesus do) as a caregiver?"

I won't speculate on what Jesus would do; I can tell you what He did do: He delegated.

When Jesus saw his mother and the disciple whom he loved standing nearby, he said to his mother, "Woman, behold, your son!" Then he said to the disciple, "Behold, your mother!" And from that hour the disciple took her to his own home. John 19:26-27 ESV

If Jesus can delegate, it stands to reason that you can enlist help in order for you to take a breather.

For to be free is not merely to cast off one's chains,
but to live in a way that respects and
enhances the freedom of others.

Nelson Mandela

———

Therefore don't worry about tomorrow,
because tomorrow will worry about itself.
Each day has enough trouble of its own.

Matthew 6:34 HCSB

Chapter 39

THEY'RE GOING TO FALL

A man's got to know his limitations.

Clint Eastwood as Dirty Harry

A woman once shared with me that she couldn't get away from her aging father because every time she left, something bad happened. "He falls each time I leave him with someone else!" she said, while tearing up in frustration.

"Something bad happens whether you are there or not," I told her. "You can't guarantee your presence will forever prohibit him from falling. If you've done your best to provide safeguards and to have someone there in the event of a fall or other mishaps, what more can you do?"

As we all struggle with the independence issue, these questions require consideration:

- Will your loved one's life improve if you are out of the picture?
- Are you able to care for them when you are emotionally and physically exhausted?
- Will they be better off once you're a "husk of a human being"?

Looking at those questions, "seeking and maintaining" a healthy level of emotional and even physical independence becomes critical not only for the caregiver but also for the patient as well. Independence is not abandonment; it's allowing a life to blossom on its own without encroachment.

I've watched my wife fall many times since she began walking on prosthetic limbs decades ago. Each time, I try to catch her if I can—and comfort her when I can't. The fact is: amputees who use prosthetic legs are going to fall. She's embarrassed when it happens, and I'm embarrassed for her. She hurts, and I hurt for her. Our sons hurt to see their mother fall. But we all recognize that for her to be who she is, she has to get back up and continue trying. That's her journey. If I, by the force of my will, tried to keep her in a wheelchair to avoid falling, I would do great harm to her—and ultimately to me. I would force her to become utterly dependent upon me and rob her of whatever level of independence she could achieve.

We're caregivers, not superheroes. We can't prevent every disaster or solve every problem. This isn't Metropolis; it's the real world. Here in the real world, they are going to fall. They will make mistakes. They will get hurt. No caregiver can eliminate those risks without endangering his or her well-being.

We do the best we can to protect the ones we love, while never forgetting that the best asset for *their* protection is to have a healthy caregiver.

Surrender to the Lord is not a tremendous sacrifice,

not an agonizing performance.

It is the most sensible thing you can do.

Corrie ten Boom

I will lift up my eyes to the hills.
From whence comes my help?
My help comes from the LORD,
Who made heaven and earth.

Psalm 121:1–2 NKJV

For what has been—thanks! For what shall be—yes!

Dag Hammarskjöld

Chapter 40

—⊰❁⊱—

THE SERENITY PRAYER

Stop quarreling with God!
If you agree with him, you will have peace at last,
and things will go well for you.

Job 22:21 NLT

The American theologian Reinhold Niebuhr composed a prayer containing one sentence that became known as the Serenity Prayer. Not limited to dealing with addiction issues, this prayer applies to every life situation—including our role as caregivers.

"God, grant me the serenity
to accept the things I cannot change,
the courage to change the things I can,
and the wisdom to know the difference."

Of course, Niebuhr's words are far easier to recite than they are to live by. But if my years as a caregiver have taught me anything, they've taught me to focus intently on the things I can change, to leave the rest up to God, and to accept His verdict *on everything*.

Everybody experiences adversity, but as caregivers, we're confronted with it every day. Some things we can control; many things we cannot.

Early in my caregiving journey, I tried to control everything. But eventually I learned that, unlike Clark Kent, I wasn't wearing Superman's cape underneath my navy blazer. There were some things I simply couldn't do. And there were some things I simply couldn't understand.

The ideal man bears the accidents of life with dignity and grace, making the best of circumstances.

Aristotle

For years, I've heard my father often share, "God's got this problem: He thinks HE's God."

When I made the decision to live out the underlying meaning of that statement, my life changed for the better. Recognizing that I am not responsible for results and other people's behaviors has imparted greater freedom to love and live without the burden of carrying something that isn't mine.

Although circumstances and challenges haven't changed, I am changing. I'm learning that I can respond without reacting. I can care for without carrying. I can be at peace in the midst of craziness.

My hope for you, as a caregiver and as a person, is that you come to terms with—and celebrate—yourself, your responsibilities, your loved ones, and your Creator. When you do, you can be comforted in the knowledge that your life as a caregiver is *both* a mission from above *and* a grand opportunity for service here below.

The first word in that prayer is "God." Just calling out is an act of faith and an admission of need. When it comes to seeking God's help, all we need is "need." We caregivers tend to push ourselves to inhuman levels before finally collapsing and admitting defeat. At that point, however, is when we can experience the grace, peace, and joy of God's presence and provision. That's the wisdom part of the prayer: realizing what we can and cannot do. We cannot change other people. We cannot change God.

We, however, can change. Our circumstances don't hold us in bondage. Those reality TV shows about cops often show criminals being arrested. Even though the bad guys struggle mightily at first, and cause all kinds of stress and pain to themselves and others, they all have one thing in common: They eventually stopped struggling. At some point their bodies simply run out of strength fighting against something bigger than themselves.

It's only a matter of time, however, before we simply give out from sheer exhaustion. We often look at a physical and/or emotional collapse as failure on our part. I say it is an opportunity for us to relinquish our faulty idea of control and step into a new life of faith and calmness.

It's at that point where we are invited to trust God for today, and ask for the strength to do what is in our power to do. We also humbly admit we are powerless and ask for the courage to accept our limits, and then ask for His wisdom to know what belongs to us and what doesn't.

That's why I borrowed the principles of "The Serenity Prayer" to write "The Caregiver's Prayer." The first time that prayer is said, it will feel awkward, and maybe even pointless.

The 1,000th time, it won't.

THE CAREGIVER'S PRAYER

© 2014 Peter W. Rosenberger

Heavenly Father, I love _____.
I have committed my life to caring for him/her,
Yet I know the task is greater than my abilities.

As I seek to help another,
I ask for strength to shoulder the burdens before me.
Yet I also ask for the wisdom to know what is mine to carry.

I ask for the courage to admit my failures and make amends.
I thank You for Your grace and mercy,
and ask that You help me daily apply it to myself
and extend it to others.

As I walk through this long valley of the shadow of death,
I ask for a deeper awareness of Your presence to calm my fears.
As I glance backwards, may I only see Your provision.
As I look forward, may my eyes see Your guidance.

May I reflect You as I minister to this one whom I love.
I pray all this in the name of Your Son, Jesus Christ,
Who laid down His own life . . . for me.

ABOUT THE AUTHOR

A lifetime of experience. A lifeline for fellow caregivers.

Michael Gomez—Gomezphotography.com

Peter Rosenberger is president of Nashville-based *Standing With Hope,* an outreach whose flagship program provides artificial limbs to people in West Africa. Host of a weekly radio program, he's also an accomplished public speaker, writer, and spokesman for the needs of America's 65 million caregivers.

His is an unparalleled journey. As his wife's sole caregiver for nearly thirty years, he has labored through a medical nightmare that has mushroomed to 78 operations, the amputation of both her legs, and $9 million in medical bills. The experience and wisdom he has gleaned gives Peter a unique and astonishing understanding of health care issues facing millions of people. But more than that, he brings unmatched empathy for the deep heart-ache that causes even the strongest to falter.

"…One joke away from being a night club act," Peter combines deep compassion with a contagious humor to bring fresh air into the painful places faced by America's caregivers.

This is Rosenberger's third book.

Additional books available through
www.standingwithhope.com

Peter Rosenberger's new app for caregivers is available on
the web and for iOS devices. View online at www.carekitapp.com
or search for **CareKit** in the AppStore.

Enter promo code "hope" for a free one-month trial.